Southern Living®

Party
Cookbook

Complete Menus and Entertaining Guide

The *Southern Living* Party Cookbook

A MODERN GUIDE TO GATHERING

ELIZABETH HEISKELL

AUTHOR OF *WHAT CAN I BRING?*

Oxmoor House®

Executive Editor: Katherine Cobbs
Project Editor: Melissa Brown
Design Director: Melissa Clark
Photo Director: Paden Reich
Designer: Matt Ryan
Photographers: Antonis Achilleos, Iain Bagwell, Caitlin Bensel, Greg DuPree, Laurey W. Glenn, Alison Miksch, Victor Protasio, Hector Manuel Sanchez
Prop Stylists: Cindy Barr, Heather Chadduck Hillegas, Lindsey Lower, Mindi Shapiro
Food Stylists: Mary Claire Britton, Margaret Monroe Dickey, Emily Nabors Hall, Anna Hampton, Chelsea Zimmer
Recipe Developers and Testers: Adam Dolge, Adam Hickman, Julia G. Levy, Pam Lolley, Kathleen Phillips, Karen Rankin, Deb Wise
Copy Editors: Ashley Strickland Freeman, Dolores Hydock
Proofreader: Donna Baldone
Indexer: Mary Ann Laurens
Fellows: Kaitlyn Pacheco, Holly Ravazzolo, Hanna Yokeley
Calligraphers: Taylor Eisenhauer, Abigail Wilt

Trade Edition
ISBN-13: 978-0-8487-5665-9

Direct Mail Edition
ISBN-13: 978-0-8487-6098-4

Library of Congress Control Number: 2018950865

First Edition 2018

Printed in the United States of America

10 9 8 7 6 5 4 3 2 1

We welcome your comments and suggestions about Time Inc. Books.

Time Inc. Books
Attention: Book Editors
P.O. Box 62310
Tampa, Florida 33662-2310
(800) 765-6400

Time Inc. Books products may be purchased for business or promotional use. For information on bulk purchases, please contact Christi Crowley in the Special Sales Department at (845) 895-9858.

This book belongs to

CONTENTS

My great-grandmother was one of the loveliest hostesses in the Delta. After her, my grandmother carried that baton—both in the Delta and abroad. It's no wonder then that my mother's parties were some of the best the state of Mississippi has ever seen. Entertaining is in my DNA just as much as the Delta is. Turns out, I discovered that many of my "family recipes" were actually from the original 1972 *Southern Living Party Cookbook*, which is the inspiration for this book. Then as now, when a great cook or host stumbles upon a terrific recipe, they often hide the source. The original *Southern Living Party Cookbook* is the best-selling *Southern Living* cookbook of all time for a reason—the delicious recipes and timeless entertaining advice that guided generations. I am beyond honored to be a part of this modern-day reinvention of that classic.

Parties are occasions that mark memories. Thanks to my family's love of entertaining, I have so many wonderful ones etched in my mind. I remember the elegant christening luncheon my grandmother hosted (though I can't remember who was christened) where I fell in love with old-fashioned Eggs Goldenrod—chopped hard-boiled eggs served on buttery toast topped with cream gravy—and rich chocolate tartlets. I heard detailed stories of how my great-grandmother turned her beautiful home on Mississippi's Lake Washington into a social club for dinner and dancing during the Depression to make ends meet.

Not to be outdone, my mother threw elaborate parties at our home in Rosedale. On one occasion, she borrowed the Macaw parrot from the John Deere dealership and put it in an enormous wrought-iron birdcage that she hung from the ancient pecan tree in our backyard. The magnificent bird was the perfect shade of green to match her Key lime silk tablecloths. Little did she know, the parrot knew only cusswords. You see, the men who hung around the tractor dealership where the bird resided had taught that parrot every cussword under the sun. That bird squawked one cussword after another from the moment guests arrived until they departed. It wasn't part of mother's vision for a perfect party, but it was without a doubt a party to remember.

Daddy is notorious for late-night dance parties, where the tunes of BB King and Jerry Lee Lewis reign. They always start innocently enough with a few people and a few cocktails and then the next thing you know the place is a juke joint teeming with revelers because Daddy doesn't know a stranger so everyone is welcome. The mess the next day does not cancel out that great time. That's why Daddy continues to party.

With all the partying I have taken part in, you'd think I would be more at ease throwing parties of my own. I have been catering since high school and have thrown thousands of parties for clients that have gone off without a hitch — except that one time. (But why bring up my mistaking a glass bottle of dish soap for olive oil and serving it to the Memphis prima ballerina on her wedding day?) Assumptions aside, when it comes to my own parties, it's often a different story.

Before my annual Christmas party I run around for days like a chicken with my head cut off. One year, I was on hands and knees rearranging lava rocks in the fireplace as guests arrived. I'd forgotten all the rules I tell my clients, like "RELAX! Your guests are your friends and just grateful to be included" and "the more relaxed you are, the more fun your guests will have" or "people make the party, not the food, flowers, or monogrammed guest towels." Bottom line: Entertaining can be daunting if you don't step back, breathe, and remember what's important. I bet some of the parties you remember included a few great friends, a bowl of nuts, and bottles of wine and you have no idea if there were scented candles or perfectly arranged fireplace logs. So let yourself off the hook.

Like the best-selling book that the lovely hostesses in my lineage turned to again and again for guidance, I have confidence that this modern-day sequel will be the gracious entertaining guide that you (and generations to come) turn to again and again. So let's get the party started!

Etiquette & Invites

The rules of etiquette are in constant evolution. The definition of an informal invitation in the original 1972 edition of the *Southern Living Party Cookbook* was described as a printed invitation that was not engraved. Today, an informal invitation might be designed and printed at home and mailed, or it might be sent in the form of a text, phone call, or email. Formal engraved invitations, on the other hand, haven't changed much. Aside from including all the necessary party details—occasion, location, date, and time—such an invitation also denotes "who" is invited (the addressee is the invited party) and whether the host requires a reply. Unless the host is a very close friend, it is not proper to ask if you may bring a guest when an invitation is addressed to you alone.

EXAMPLES

Mr. Simon Smith = Invitation for 1

Dr. Sarah and Mr. Simon Smith = Invitation for 2

Dr. Sarah Smith and Guest = Invitation for 1 or 2

10

Whether an invitation arrives electronically or in the mail, if a response is requested, the proper thing to do is to reply within a day or two of receipt and definitely before a given deadline.

RSVP *Répondez s'il vous plait* or Please reply. Let the host know if you will or will not attend.

REGRETS ONLY Let the host know only if you are unable to attend, and by the method noted—phone or email. If no contact information is provided, your regret by handwritten note to the host is expected within a day or two.

RESPONSE CARD Fill in and return the card by the date noted.

NO RESPONSE CARD Formal invitation without a response card requires a written reply to the host within a day or two of receipt.

NO EXCEPTIONS

Don't be a no-show! Honor your reply. Cancel after accepting only if faced with an unavoidable, unforeseen circumstance and do so graciously by phone.

Buffet Feng Shui

Mixing and mingling is the essence of a great party, so don't let a buffet line traffic jam put the brakes on a good time. Filling a plate should not necessitate a roadmap or compass. A clearly defined start to the line and well-defined order of dishes go a long way to making navigating the noshes a no-brainer.

VARY THE HEIGHTS Stack books beneath table linens or use pedestals to elevate some dishes for easier access and to add a little design panache.

SIGNAL THE START A stack of plates is a visual cue for the start of any buffet line. If the setup is on a table, pull it out from the wall so traffic can flow down both sides.

IDENTIFY DISHES A menu card at the start of the buffet, or individual place cards identifying each dish and any need-to-know information for guests (contains peanuts, for example), helps keep the line moving.

SAVE UTENSILS FOR LAST Arrange napkins and silverware at the end of the buffet so guests won't have to juggle them while filling plates.

GIVE SOME SUPPORT An empty saucer next to each dish gives guests a spot to rest serving spoons and protects Grandma's heirloom sideboard or dining table.

11

POSITION STRATEGICALLY Place food you have limited supply of at the end of the line. Guests will be less tempted to take a giant scoop when their plate is nearly full.

A Glass for Every Toast

Stocking a bar with the ideal assortment of glassware takes restraint. There are so many options in different shapes, sizes, and materials that it's easy to go from conservative collector of bar basics to "I-just-have-to-have-it" hoarder. Do you really need ceramic totem mugs from Samoa or stemmed coconut cups from Tonga? In addition to the standard 8-ounce and 16-ounce glasses you most likely have in your cabinet, stick only to specialty glasses you know you will use from the list below. Many can be enlisted for use in numerous ways.

BASICS

8-ounce glasses
(Old-Fashioned/Rocks)

16-ounce glasses
(Highball/Collins/Pint)

SPECIALTY GLASSES (FROM LEFT TO RIGHT)

Irish Coffee Mugs	Brandy Snifters
Cocktail Glasses (Martini)	Burgundy Glasses
Sherry Glasses	Champagne Flutes
Red Wineglasses	Moscow Mule Mugs
White Wineglasses	Margarita Glasses (or Coupe glasses)
Champagne Tulip Glasses	

12

TOASTING TIPS

RULE #1 BE BRIEF

It's best to keep a toast under two or three minutes.

RULE #2 REHEARSE

Sometimes even spontaneity requires a little forethought. Practice out loud in the mirror a few times for the benefit of all.

RULE #3 GET (AND KEEP) THE CROWD'S ATTENTION

Avoid tapping your glass for attention. Simply stand and speak loudly and clearly.

RULE #4 DON'T DRINK TO YOURSELF

Avoid raising your glass, and remain seated, when the toast is offered to you.

RULE #5 LET THE HOST TOAST FIRST

Champagne glasses on the table indicate toasts will be made, but it's traditionally reserved for the dessert course.

RULE #6 NEVER REFUSE TO PARTICIPATE

If you're a nondrinker, it is courteous to raise an empty glass, rather than none at all. If you're nervous about public speaking, have a couple of short toasts committed to memory in case you're unexpectedly called upon.

RULE #7 INFORM GUESTS IF YOU WOULD LIKE THEM TO TOAST

If you're hosting a formal party or wedding and would like for certain guests to toast the honorees, it's polite to call them a week before the party to let them know so they may be thoughtfully prepared.

butter plate   flowers

red

dessert spoon

dessert fork

white   water

butter knife

salad fork   dinner fork   salad plate   dinner knife   soup spoon

fish fork   dinner plate   charger   fish knife

Setting the Table

Large or small, formal or casual, seated gatherings are special occasions. A well-set table is like the perfect outfit. It makes a statement. Whether you're hosting a barbecue shindig with paper plates and plastic cutlery or a five-course dinner with wine pairings, setting the table with all the necessary pieces sets a tone—laid-back and casual or elegant and impressive. It makes a meal more enjoyable for your guests from start to finish, too, when all the necessary utensils are at hand. The setup above is the formula for an all-out formal feast. Simply subtract the pieces you do not need for your occasion.

Gifts for the Host and Parting Favors

Whether you're a cocktail hour, dinner party, or a weekend guest, never show up empty-handed. Gifts need not be expensive, just thoughtful. Give a small token that fits the theme, location, host, or has a story.

EXAMPLES

HOST'S HOBBY OR PASSION (FOR THE GARDENER OR COOK)

Potted globe basil plant or cellophane bag of toasted pecans with a recipe card attached (example: Southern Pecan-Basil Pesto)

PERSONAL MEANING YOU WISH TO CONVEY (YOU'RE A BEEKEEPER)

Honey from your hives in a jar with your label and a ribbon attaching a wooden honey dripper

15

PARTY THEME (CHRISTMAS CAROLING PARTY)

Hot cocoa mix + marshmallows

LOCALE (BONFIRE ON THE BEACH)

Turkish beach towel

PARTY RULE NO. 1

No returns accepted (or expected)

Bring party hosts an appetizer on a keep-it platter—or flowers in a keep-it vase. Or take a breakfast nibble to help with the morning after.

Estimating Quantities

BEVERAGE ESTIMATION

If what your guests might choose to drink is a mystery, it's best to estimate amounts for each type of beverage below based on the assumption that everyone at the party will drink it. That way you may have leftovers of one or more of the below at the end of the party, but most likely will not run out of something mid-party. It's safe to count on about three drinks per person for a 2 ½-hour party.

BEVERAGES (FOR A 2 ½-HOUR PARTY)

Ice: 1 pound per person

Sodas and Mixers: 3 per guest

Beer: 3 (12-ounce bottles) per guest

Wine: 2 (750-milliliter) bottles for every 3 guests (4 glasses per bottle)

Spirits: 1 (750-milliliter) bottle for every 4 to 5 guests (16 drinks per bottle with 1 ½-ounce pours)

FOOD ESTIMATION

You know your crowd, so adjust the ranges below accordingly. It's always wise to round up when estimating to play it safe.

HORS D'OEUVRES

Plan on a well-rounded variety of 3 to 8 different appetizers, considering the length of your party. (For example, based on the below, you would need 1 or 2 passed canapés or appetizers that yield enough for guests to have 2 to 3 bites in total before a buffet or seated dinner.) Always vary ingredient types, textures, and colors for interest and be sure not to duplicate elements that might appear on the buffet or table.

1 to 2 appetizers to yield 2 to 3 bites per guest before a meal is to be served

2 to 3 appetizers to yield 4 to 6 bites per person at a cocktail party where guests are set to depart early (4 to 6 p.m.) and a meal is not being served

3 to 4 appetizers to yield 6 bites per person for a cocktail party that bridges the dinner hour (6 to 8 p.m.), but a meal is not being served

4 to 6 appetizers to yield 8 to 10 bites per person to serve as a meal when a cocktail party spans an evening

MAIN DISHES

Protein: 6 to 8 ounces per person

Vegetables: 3 ½ ounces per person

Potatoes: 5 ounces per person

Rice and Grains: 1 ½ to 2 ounces per person as a side dish; 3 ounces per person for a main course like paella or risotto

Pasta: 2 ounces for a side dish and 4 ounces for a main dish per person

Green Salad: 1 ounce undressed greens per person

DESSERTS

2 to 3 bite-size desserts, cookies, or petits fours

1 (2- to 3-inch) wedge cake or pie

4 to 5 ounces creamy dessert, such as pudding, mousse, or ice cream

Teas, Coffees, and Receptions

Petits fours, finger sandwiches, and coffee punch. . .these are a few of my favorite things, but first, some guidelines. When planning a reception, remember to keep it light and fun. There's no need to overwhelm your guests with a massive food display. These parties are held between meal times so you're only required to provide a few nibbles. The good news is that with the extra time you'll have, you can spend more time preparing delicate canapés and beautiful sweets to make your guests swoon.

Champagne Punch
Chicken Salad Pastry Shells
Mixed Nuts

Champagne Punch
Chicken Salad Pastry Shells
Garlicky Mixed Nuts

SIP and SEE

Thumbprint Cheese Wafers
with Pecans

Sugar Cookies with
Royal Icing

SIP AND SEE

MENU FOR 12

Sip and see says it all. This party is all about getting together with friends and family and oohing and aahing. What in the world are we oohing and aahing over you might ask?

Well, when I got married all my wedding gifts were displayed in my grandmother's sunroom. Tables were brought in and shelving was erected. Yards of tulle were made into bunting. Silk tablecloths were draped. Needless to say, it was a big production.

My grandmother did this for my mother and her mother did it for her when she married. Although it seemed very strange to me, I didn't dare question such an enduring tradition. By the time Luke and I were married, my grandmother's house looked like the housewares department at Neiman Marcus. To top it all off, my grandmother organized a beautiful sip and see for all of her friends to come over and peruse the gifts.

My grandmother's closest friends came, had Champagne punch, a light bite, and a good look. I loved the idea of a sip and see, but since I wasn't planning on getting married again I needed to figure out something else we could celebrate with a formal look-see! Then the perfect occasion fell into my lap: My friend who was having her third baby really didn't want or need a baby shower so instead we waited for the baby to be born and then invited friends and family to ooh and aah over the precious infant.

I think my favorite sip and see was held by a friend who had a new boyfriend who'd moved to town, so we decided to have a sip and see Rudy. It was just the silliest fun ever. Let your imagination run wild!

Champagne Punch

HANDS-ON **20 MINUTES**   TOTAL **20 MINUTES**   SERVES **24**

Feel free to select a sherbet that will coordinate with the flowers or the tablecloths when making this punch. Sparkling wine is a blank canvas that will pair easily with any flavor. I recommend using Champagne coupes that are as in now as they were in the '70s.

1 ½ cups (about 6 ounces)
   powdered sugar

½ cup (4 ounces) orange liqueur
   (such as Triple Sec)

½ cup (4 ounces) cognac

½ cup maraschino cherry juice

1 quart pineapple sherbet

3 (750-milliliter) bottles sparkling
   wine or Champagne, chilled

1 orange, sliced (optional)

1 lemon, sliced (optional)

Stir together the sugar and orange liqueur thoroughly in a pitcher until the sugar is dissolved, about 1 minute. Stir in the cognac and cherry juice. Pour into a chilled punch bowl; gently place the block of sherbet in the center. Slowly add the sparkling wine, and garnish with the orange and lemon slices, if desired. (Do not stir the punch after the sparkling wine is added or it will lose its sparkle.)

Note

If it's a warm day and you're hosting
a convivial crowd, it might be wise
to be prepared for refills. Count on
8 ounces per guest.

Chicken Salad Pastry Shells

HANDS-ON **25 MINUTES**   TOTAL **2 HOURS, 30 MINUTES**   SERVES **12**

I wish I knew how many variations of chicken salad there are. Curried, with nuts, with fruit, with nuts and fruit . . . I could go on for days. I have known people to come to blows over which recipe is the best. I honestly cannot say which spin gets my vote, but I can say don't ever, and I mean ever, use dark meat in your chicken salad.

2 (10-ounce) packages frozen puff
  pastry shells

½ cup mayonnaise

½ cup sour cream

2 tablespoons chopped fresh tarragon

2 teaspoons lemon zest plus 1 tablespoon
  fresh juice (from 1 lemon)

½ teaspoon kosher salt

¼ teaspoon black pepper

4 cups chopped cooked chicken

1 ½ cups (about 9 ounces) diced sweet
  crisp apple (such as Gala, Honeycrisp,
  or Fuji)

1 cup diced celery (from 2 stalks)

3 tablespoons finely chopped red onion

1 cup slivered toasted almonds

1 Bake the pastry shells according to the package directions; cool completely, about 20 minutes.

2 Whisk together the mayonnaise, sour cream, tarragon, lemon zest, lemon juice, salt, and pepper in a large bowl. Stir in the chicken, apple, celery, and onion just until combined. Cover and chill at least 2 hours and up to 24 hours.

3 Stir in ¾ cup of the almonds just before serving, and divide evenly between the baked pastry shells (about ¼ cup per shell). Sprinkle evenly with the remaining ¼ cup almonds.

Garlicky Mixed Nuts

(photograph on page 23)

HANDS-ON **10 MINUTES**   TOTAL **10 MINUTES**   SERVES **12**

Every evening my grandmother and her best friend, Mrs. Shelton, sat and drank cocktails and gossiped for hours. I can remember one particular day when they talked about a hostess in town who invited them over for drinks and hors d'oeuvres, but when they arrived she put out only a bowl of nuts. Mrs. Shelton kept saying, "Not even a cheese ball! She could have at least put out some cream cheese and pepper jelly. Lord, you don't even have to cook that." The list of dishes that she could have prepared went on and on. They talked about that poor woman and her nuts for days. I must say that these garlicky nuts, with their fresh herbs, orange zest, and raisins, might even impress Mrs. Shelton and "MeMa."

1 cup chopped pecans

½ cup pine nuts

½ cup sliced almonds

½ cup blanched hazelnuts

⅔ cup olive oil

1 cup chopped fresh flat-leaf parsley

⅔ cup golden raisins

4 teaspoons chopped fresh thyme

2 teaspoons loosely packed orange zest

1 teaspoon crushed red pepper

½ teaspoon table salt

2 large garlic cloves, sliced

Cook the pecans, pine nuts, almonds, and hazelnuts in hot olive oil in a medium skillet over medium, stirring constantly, 2 minutes or until toasted. Remove from the heat. Stir in the parsley, raisins, thyme, orange zest, crushed red pepper, salt, and sliced garlic. Pour the mixture into 2 (8-ounce) jars. Store in the refrigerator up to 2 weeks. Remove the garlic before serving.

PARTY RULE NO. 2

No dish is "to die for"!

Milk, soy, eggs, wheat, peanuts, tree nuts, fish, and shellfish are the most common food allergies in adults. When inviting guests to a party, ask about food allergies and plan the menu accordingly. If you are invited to a party, share your food sensitivities with the host and offer to contribute a dish of your own to the menu.

Thumbprint Cheese Wafers with Pecans

(photograph on page 23)

HANDS-ON **20 MINUTES**   TOTAL **1 HOUR, 35 MINUTES (PER BATCH)**   SERVES **18**

This recipe is very simple to put together but not so simple to bake. You don't want to put these wafers in the oven and then do two loads of laundry, talk on the phone, or clean your car. You must keep an eye on them. It is also a good idea to rotate the pan in the middle of baking to ensure that the edges don't burn. Substitute most any favorite jam or jelly here.

2 ¼ cups (about 9 ⅝ ounces)
    all-purpose flour

1 (8-ounce) block sharp Cheddar
    cheese, shredded

1 cup (8 ounces) salted butter,
    softened and cut into 1-inch pieces

1 ½ cups finely chopped pecans

3 tablespoons hot pepper jelly

1   Pulse the flour, cheese, and butter in a food processor at 5-second intervals until the dough forms a ball, about 1 minute. Shape tablespoons of dough into 1-inch balls and roll each in the chopped pecans. Place the balls 2 inches apart on baking sheets lined with parchment paper. Press a thumb in the center of each to make an indentation. Chill for at least 30 minutes before baking.

2   Preheat the oven to 350°F. Bake in the preheated oven, in batches, until light golden brown, 15 to 18 minutes. You may need to gently press the indentation again (with a thumb of steel) when these first come out of the oven. Transfer the thumbprints to wire racks; cool completely, about 30 minutes. Spoon about ¼ teaspoon jelly into each indentation.

Sugar Cookies with Royal Icing

HANDS-ON **10 MINUTES**   TOTAL **10 MINUTES**   SERVES **30**

A lovely cookie, monogrammed with royal icing, is a detail your guests won't soon forget. I suggest trying this process only after you have placed an order for them with your local bakery. This is what I like to call the "plan b" order. I won't lie, this recipe takes practice and it's not as easy as it looks. For my daughter's third birthday, I wanted to serve sugar cookies with royal icing that were shaped like farm animals. After I found out my local bakery charged two dollars per cookie, I decided to make them myself. Days passed, my kitchen was covered in royal icing, and the farm animals looked like watery trolls. I finally gave up, called the bakery, and begged them to make the expensive-for-good-reason cookies for the birthday celebration.

1 (16-ounce) package powdered sugar

3 tablespoons meringue powder (such as Wilton)

6 to 8 tablespoons warm water

2 ½ dozen (3-inch) sugar cookies

1 Beat the powdered sugar, meringue powder, and 6 tablespoons of the water with an electric mixer at low speed until blended. Beat at high speed 4 minutes or until stiff peaks form. Add up to 2 tablespoons additional water, ¼ teaspoon at a time, until the desired consistency is reached.

2 Spoon the icing into a piping bag and pipe desired design onto cookies. Let stand until the icing hardens.

Note

Use less water for a stiff icing that's
perfect for attaching cookies to cake stands.
Use more water for thinner icing suitable
for piping delicate designs on cookies.

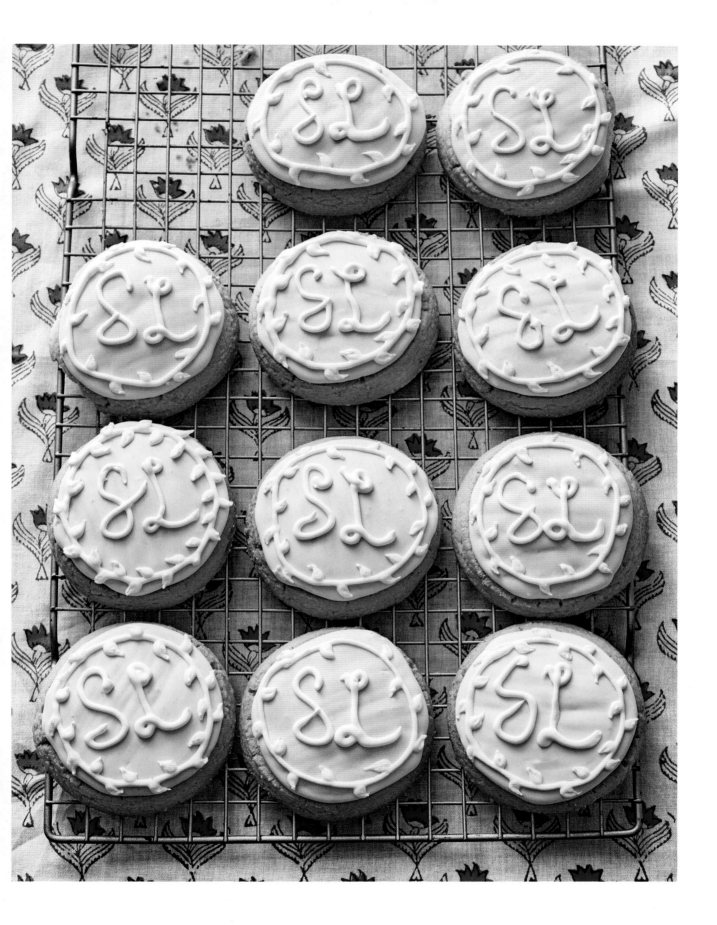

GRADUATION COFFEE

Completing 12 years of school is a huge accomplishment (as is completing college or graduate school). The years have been filled with hard work, countless laughs, pranks, dress-up days, drama, football games, disappointments, and triumphs. Graduation is cause for celebration. When planning graduation parties, keep in mind the age of the honorees and their friends. High school graduates may be ready to fly, but they are well under the legal drinking age so serving alcohol is a never! This party tops the list as a perfect way to honor your young adult. Coffee shops are the drive-in diners and soda fountains of my youth. The lines in coffee shops are long for a reason. Since the cool and not-so-cool kids hang out there for hours before and after school, they've become young coffee connoisseurs.

When planning your graduation coffee, consider hiring a barista from your local coffee shop. There are lots of syrups and flavorings that they can provide to add variety and another level of excitement. At my local Oxford farmers' market, an adorable girl sells freshly brewed specialty coffees out of a converted VW bus. She can park her coffee-shop-on-wheels anywhere—even your driveway—so guests can place orders for their favorite concoctions. Triple decaf no-foam latte with caramel drizzle, anyone? You got it!

Set tables and food outside for an outdoor café soirée. Order printed coffee cups with the graduates' names, monograms, or a single inspirational phrase. Ask the hostesses to collect vintage coffee cups for the party, and then fill the cups with chocolate-covered espresso beans and wrap the filled cups in cellophane bags tied with ribbon. I cannot think of a more adorable and delicious take-home happy! Follow these fun steps and your party will rival the best coffee shop in town.

Dark Chocolate Chai Latte

HANDS-ON **20 MINUTES**   TOTAL **30 MINUTES**   SERVES **24**

I have to be honest. I strongly believe that coffee has a flavor: coffee. There is no reason to go mucking it up with caramel, pumpkin spice, or hazelnut. Since there are thousands of coffee shops that sell millions of specialty coffees, I am obviously in the minority. So as hard as it is for me to endorse this latte, I will. Ultimately, entertaining is about pleasing your guests. It is not always about your likes or dislikes.

12 cups whole milk

3 cups whipping cream

1 ½ cups packed light brown sugar

12 ounces dark chocolate, chopped

1 (3-inch) piece fresh ginger, peeled and sliced

18 cardamom seeds

3 whole star anise

¾ teaspoon whole cloves

¾ teaspoon ground cinnamon

¾ teaspoon black peppercorns

6 cups water

12 regular-size tea bags

1 Bring the milk, whipping cream, brown sugar, chocolate, ginger, cardamom, star anise, cloves, cinnamon, peppercorns, and 6 cups water to a boil in a Dutch oven or large stockpot over medium-high, stirring occasionally until the chocolate is melted. Add the tea bags; cover, reduce the heat to low, and simmer 10 minutes.

2 Pour the mixture through a fine mesh strainer into a heatproof pitcher, discarding the solids. Serve warm or chilled over ice.

Petite Cinnamon Rolls

HANDS-ON **30 MINUTES**   TOTAL **1 HOUR, 22 MINUTES**   SERVES **24**

When serving a breakfast, brunch, or coffee, it is important to have a little sweet bite to round out the menu. As a rule, I don't serve desserts before 11 a.m., but this petite cinnamon roll is the perfect way to satisfy any sweet tooth. Frankly, no occasion exists where it is a good idea to serve a cinnamon roll that is as big as a hubcap. I am not saying don't buy hubcap cinnamon rolls, but please enjoy them in the privacy of your own home.

1 (16-ounce) package hot roll mix
  (such as Pillsbury)

6 tablespoons (3 ounces) salted
  butter, softened

½ cup granulated sugar

½ cup packed light brown sugar

1 teaspoon ground cinnamon

2 cups (about 8 ounces) powdered sugar

¼ cup whole milk

½ teaspoon vanilla extract

1 Prepare the hot roll mix dough according to the package directions. Divide the dough into 2 equal portions. Roll each dough portion into a 12- x 8-inch rectangle on a lightly floured surface. Spread each with 3 tablespoons of the butter.

2 Stir together the granulated sugar, brown sugar, and cinnamon; sprinkle half of the sugar mixture over each buttered dough rectangle. Roll up each rectangle starting at 1 long side.

3 Cut each rolled dough portion into 24 (½-inch) slices. Place the slices, cut sides up, in cups of 2 lightly greased 24-cup miniature muffin pans. Cover with plastic wrap, and let rise in a warm place (80° to 85°F), free from drafts, about 30 minutes.

4 Preheat the oven to 375°F. Bake the rolls in the preheated oven until golden brown, about 12 to 15 minutes, rotating pans after 10 minutes. Transfer the rolls from pans to wire racks, and let cool 10 minutes.

5 Stir together the powdered sugar, milk, and vanilla until smooth. Spread over the tops of the rolls.

Fruit & Mint Skewers

(photograph on page 39)

HANDS-ON **30 MINUTES**   TOTAL **1 HOUR, 15 MINUTES**   SERVES **24**

When making fruit skewers always pick fruit that is in season. A watermelon is not going to be good in February. Even if you use a melon baller to make a perfect watermelon ball, put it on an adorable bamboo skewer, and douse it in mint syrup, you are just putting lipstick on the proverbial pig.

1 ½ cups white balsamic vinegar

1 ½ tablespoons honey

48 (1-inch) cubes watermelon
(about 3 cups)

48 (1-inch) cubes honeydew melon
(about 3 cups)

48 (1-inch) cubes cantaloupe
(about 3 cups)

15 ounces feta cheese, cut into
1-inch cubes

96 small- to medium-size mint leaves
(about 1- to 1 ½-inch-long leaves)

½ teaspoon black pepper

1 Stir together the vinegar and honey in a small saucepan over medium-high. Bring the mixture to a boil; reduce the heat to low, and simmer, stirring occasionally, until the mixture thickens and reduces to about ⅓ cup, about 15 minutes. Remove from the heat, and cool completely, about 30 minutes.

2 Thread 3 assorted melon cubes, 1 feta cube, and 2 mint leaves on each of 48 (3-inch) wooden skewers. Brush the skewers with the vinegar reduction, and sprinkle with the pepper. Serve well chilled.

Sausage Balls

(photograph on page 39)

HANDS-ON **20 MINUTES**   TOTAL **35 MINUTES**   SERVES **48**

It's hard to describe the perfection of this three-ingredient classic. Guests of all ages will light up with delight when they see this treat at your next brunch, breakfast, or tailgate. Instead of using regular Cheddar cheese, try substituting your favorite pimiento cheese recipe for a fun twist on a classic.

3 cups all-purpose baking mix (such as Bisquick Original Pancake & Baking Mix)

1 (1-pound) package hot ground pork sausage

1 (10-ounce) block sharp Cheddar cheese, shredded

Preheat the oven to 400°F. Combine all the ingredients in a large bowl, pressing the mixture together with your hands. Shape into ¾-inch balls, and place on lightly greased baking sheets. Bake in the preheated oven for 15 to 18 minutes or until lightly browned.

Note

Freeze the uncooked Sausage Balls, if desired. Bake the frozen balls at 400°F for 18 to 20 minutes or until lightly browned.

Party Ham Sandwiches

HANDS-ON **10 MINUTES**   TOTAL **25 MINUTES**   SERVES **24**

This is one of those recipes that regardless of how many you make there will never be enough. They will literally disappear before your eyes. The melted spicy butter with the ham and Swiss cheese is a proven irresistible combination.

½ cup (4 ounces) salted butter, softened

½ small onion, minced

1 ½ teaspoons poppy seeds

1 teaspoon Dijon mustard

½ teaspoon Worcestershire sauce

2 (24-ounce) packages sweet dinner rolls (such as King's Hawaiian)

1 pound thinly sliced deli ham, chopped

6 ounces Swiss cheese slices

1 Preheat the oven to 350°F. Beat the butter, onion, poppy seeds, mustard, and Worcestershire sauce with an electric mixer at medium speed until blended.

2 Remove the rolls from the packages. (Do not separate the rolls.) Cut the rolls in half horizontally, creating 1 top and 1 bottom per package. Return the bottom halves of the rolls to the pans; spread the butter mixture evenly over the bottom halves.

3 Top with the ham, cheese, and remaining halves of rolls. Bake in the preheated oven for 15 minutes.

Welcome Tea

Peach Iced Tea
Pimiento Cheese Biscuits with Ham
Classic Homemade Mayonnaise
Crudités with Curry Sauce
Cream Cheese-and-Pecan
Rolled Grapes

WELCOME TEA

When we moved to Oxford, I arrived in a puddle of tears. You would have thought I moved as far away as Mexico. I was still in the same area code and could get back to my beloved Delta in an hour and a half, but none of this comforted me at all. I missed my friends, I missed my church, I missed my home, I missed my Kroger, and I missed everything familiar. One of my best friends from childhood, Vontese, moved to Oxford years before and was kind enough to have a welcome tea for me. She was brilliant! She decided that I should cook all of the food so people could be introduced to both me and my catering company.

On paper the idea was wonderful, but sheer terror set in on the day of the party. It was intimidating enough to be introduced to so many strangers, but it was terrifying to introduce my food as well. As usual, all my worries were for nothing. Vontese's friends embraced my business and me with open arms. Vontese has always been my creative friend and not much has changed over the years. For the party, she hand-made little boxes to hold the cupcakes. The boxes were tied with a ribbon and card including my name, address, email address, my husband's name, the names and ages of my children, and from where I had moved. I thought this was such a fun takeaway to help people connect with me. That party helped dry my tears and was responsible for my adjustment to my new hometown.

Peach Iced Tea

HANDS-ON **5 MINUTES**   TOTAL **5 MINUTES**   SERVES **14 TO 16**

I love to serve this tea in the summer, but you can serve it any time of year. Canned peach nectar is a great way to impart sweet peachy flavor and makes this tea a crowd-pleasing start to a party.

3 (11.5-ounce) cans peach nectar

8 cups prepared unsweetened tea

1 cup granulated sugar or to taste

¼ cup fresh lemon juice (from 1 lemon)

Stir together all the ingredients in a large pitcher; chill until ready to serve.

PARTY RULE NO. 3

Ask not what your host can do for you...

Make refills DIY so guests don't have to ask. Set up drink stations in rooms people use most so that they can help themselves. A tea towel-lined tray is the perfect place for emptied glasses. Your party setup should be both easy for guests to navigate and easy on you, so you can join in the fun with your guests too.

Pimiento Cheese Biscuits with Ham

HANDS-ON **35 MINUTES**   TOTAL **1 HOUR**   SERVES **15**

A client from New York City called needing catering help for a literacy tour she oversaw. One of the tour highlights was a cocktail reception on the grounds of Rowan Oak (William Faulkner's family home). I began to list all of the lovely hors d'oeuvres and delightful Southern fare we would serve that surely Faulkner himself would approve of, but when I mentioned pimiento cheese biscuits, she said she had never heard of "mento biscuits." I repeated "pimiento cheese biscuits" and after about three minutes of repeating it, I finally spelled it out, assuming we had a bad connection. It was then she explained she had no idea what pimiento cheese was. (Bless her heart!) I looked around the room for cameras, assuming that I was being pranked on one of those funny TV shows. As soon as she crossed the Mason-Dixon Line, I met her with a pint of pimiento cheese and saltine crackers, and as you might expect, it was love at first bite!

4 ounces sharp Cheddar cheese, shredded (about 1 cup)

2 ¼ cups (about 9 ounces) self-rising soft-wheat flour (such as White Lily Self-Rising Soft Wheat Flour)

½ cup (4 ounces) cold salted butter

1 cup whole buttermilk

1 (4-ounce) jar diced pimientos, undrained

Self-rising soft-wheat flour

2 tablespoons (1 ounce) salted butter, melted

Classic Homemade Mayonnaise (page 46)

1 pound thinly sliced country ham

1 Combine the Cheddar cheese and flour in a large bowl. Cut the cold butter into ¼-inch-thick slices. Sprinkle the butter slices over the flour mixture, and toss. Cut the butter into the flour mixture with a pastry blender until crumbly and mixture resembles small peas. Cover and chill 10 minutes.

2 Preheat the oven to 450°F. Combine the buttermilk and pimientos; add the buttermilk mixture to the flour mixture, stirring just until the dry ingredients are moistened.

3 Turn the dough out onto a floured surface; knead 3 or 4 times, adding additional flour as needed. With floured hands, pat the dough into a ¾-inch-thick rectangle (9 x 5 inches). Sprinkle the top with additional flour. Fold the dough over onto itself in 3 sections, starting with 1 short end, as if folding a letter. Repeat the process 2 more times, beginning with pressing into a ¾-inch-thick dough rectangle (about 9 x 5 inches).

4 Pat the dough to ½-inch thickness on a floured surface; cut into 2-inch rounds, and place rounds, side by side but not touching, on a parchment paper-lined jelly-roll pan. Bake in the preheated oven for 13 to 15 minutes or until lightly browned. Remove and brush with the 2 tablespoons of melted butter.

5 To assemble, split the biscuits and spread with the mayonnaise. Top the bottom halves with the ham, and replace the biscuit tops. Serve warm or at room temperature.

Classic Homemade Mayonnaise

HANDS-ON **5 MINUTES**   TOTAL **5 MINUTES**   SERVES **15**

The hallmark of a great hostess is considering every single detail of the party. The addition of homemade mayonnaise on the ham biscuits is lovely. There are store-bought brands of mayonnaise that are just fine, but in this instance, "fine" be damned. We want nothing but fabulousness. While it takes a little more effort, this recipe can be prepared days ahead to make fabulous effortless.

2 pasteurized egg yolks

1 teaspoon water

1 teaspoon white wine vinegar

1 teaspoon fresh lemon juice (from 1 lemon)

$\frac{1}{2}$ teaspoon kosher salt

$\frac{1}{4}$ teaspoon onion powder

$\frac{1}{4}$ teaspoon Dijon mustard

$\frac{1}{4}$ teaspoon hot sauce

$\frac{1}{8}$ teaspoon granulated sugar

1 cup canola oil

Beat the egg yolks, water, vinegar, lemon juice, salt, onion powder, mustard, hot sauce, and sugar with an electric mixer at high speed, using the whisk attachment, 15 seconds or until combined. With the mixer running, add the oil in a very slow, steady stream, beating until the mixture is smooth and thickened. Add additional water, 1 teaspoon at a time, to thin as desired. Refrigerate up to 3 days.

Note

Aside from the freshest eggs and the painstakingly slow addition of oil to the egg yolk mixture, the trick to foolproof homemade mayonnaise is that seemingly boring teaspoon of water mixed into the yolks at the very start. It is key to stabilizing the emulsion.

Crudités with Curry Sauce

(photograph on page 44)

HANDS-ON **30 MINUTES**   TOTAL **1 HOUR, 30 MINUTES**   SERVES **14**

Crudités is a fancy term for a beautiful raw vegetable platter often served with a vinaigrette or dip. For the best flavor, try to use vegetables that are in season. One thing I've learned over the years catering is that very few people enjoy raw broccoli or cauliflower, so take the time to blanch them quickly to make them more appealing.

1 (8-ounce) container sour cream

½ cup mayonnaise

2 tablespoons fresh lemon juice (from 1 lemon)

2 tablespoons grated onion

2 tablespoons finely chopped fresh flat-leaf parsley

1 tablespoon minced fresh chives

2 teaspoons yellow mustard

1 teaspoon curry powder

½ teaspoon paprika

½ teaspoon dried tarragon, crushed (or 1 teaspoon finely chopped fresh tarragon)

½ teaspoon table salt

¼ teaspoon black pepper, plus more for sprinkling

⅛ teaspoon hot sauce (such as Tabasco)

Sliced scallions (optional)

Assorted raw and blanched vegetables (such as cauliflower florets, sliced yellow squash, cucumber slices, celery sticks, and carrot sticks)

Stir together all the ingredients except the vegetables in a medium bowl. Cover and chill at least 1 hour or until ready to serve. Sprinkle the sauce with black pepper and sliced scallions, if desired. Serve with the assorted raw and blanched vegetables.

Cream Cheese-and-Pecan Rolled Grapes

HANDS-ON **45 MINUTES**   TOTAL **1 HOUR, 45 MINUTES**   SERVES **20 TO 25**

I have made thousands of these. I love watching my unsuspecting guests bite into one and discover the grape. As soon as the grape is crushed in their mouth, their eyes widen and a smile comes over their face. One helpful hint is to mix the grapes in the softened cream cheese then pull out a grape from the cheese and roll.

½ (8-ounce) package cream cheese, softened

2 ounces soft blue cheese, crumbled (about ½ cup)

2 to 3 tablespoons heavy cream

2 cups finely chopped toasted pecans

3 bacon slices, cooked and finely chopped

3 tablespoons finely chopped fresh flat-leaf parsley

½ pound large seedless red grapes (about 40 to 50 grapes)

1 Line a rimmed baking sheet with wax paper. Beat the cream cheese, blue cheese, and 2 tablespoons of the heavy cream in a medium bowl with an electric mixer at medium speed until smooth, about 1 minute, adding the remaining 1 tablespoon heavy cream, 1 teaspoon at a time, if needed, to reach a creamy consistency.

2 Combine the pecans, bacon, and parsley in a shallow dish. Heavily coat the grapes with the cream cheese mixture, and roll in the pecan mixture. Place on the prepared baking sheet, and chill 1 hour.

FAREWELL
COFFEE

Coffee Bar

Coffee Milk Punch

Bacon Waffles with
Pecan Chicken Tenders

Sausage & Grits
Quiches

FAREWELL COFFEE

I've worked with brides and their parents for years to plan one day. Every single aspect is thought through and labored over. We discuss table placement, color palette, menu, dish and platter styles, late-night food—you name it, we discuss it. My team strives to make sure each couple's wedding day is perfect.

I'd dreamed about my own wedding since I was a little girl. When I was eight, I watched wide-eyed from the edge of my grandparents' couch as Lady Diana married Prince Charles. I decided right then that I would settle for nothing less than the royal treatment on my big day. When I met Luke and figured out he was the one, I planned for a solid year. It consumed me, and I loved every minute of it. Our wedding was magical, and when it was over I was crushed. I cried all through the airport as we headed to our dream honeymoon. After we got settled on the plane, Luke tried to make me feel better by explaining that we were now newlyweds, which was just as special as being a bride. I had just started to perk up when the flight attendant asked passengers to raise their hands if they'd gotten married that weekend. I'll be darned if the entire plane didn't raise their hands. I burst into tears all over again.

I needed only one more day of being the bride. A farewell coffee would have been the perfect transition. It's a chance for the happy couple to gather with friends and family and reminisce about the wedding. It's so fun to talk about guests who were overserved or the bridesmaid and groomsman who made a love connection. It's also a way to extend the very special weekend. Make sure to include plenty of filling, hangover-helper recipes. Some guests may be able to stop by only for a quick hug and farewell, so have small to-go boxes ready for guests to enjoy as they travel home. If there is a ton of wedding cake left, bring it to the party and offer guests wedges to take home to enjoy. Just be sure to freeze a portion for the bride and groom to share on their first anniversary.

Coffee Milk Punch

HANDS-ON **5 MINUTES**   TOTAL **15 MINUTES**   SERVES **8**

Amanda and I were the party-throwing dynamic duo. One of my favorites was an annual Easter egg hunt. We had precious children from all over the Delta dressed in their finest bonnets and lace. We served this coffee punch in my mother-in-law's punch bowl and it was just stunning.

6 cups strong brewed hot coffee

½ cup hot fudge topping

¼ cup granulated sugar

2 cups half-and-half

1 tablespoon vanilla extract

1 cup bourbon (optional)

1 Whisk together the hot coffee, fudge topping, and sugar in a large Dutch oven until smooth. Add the half-and-half and vanilla, stirring until blended.

2 Bring the mixture to a simmer over medium-high. Remove from the heat and add the bourbon, if desired. Serve immediately, or let cool; cover and chill 1 to 24 hours, and serve over ice.

Note

Instead of using regular ice cubes in the milk punch, make an extra batch of the milk punch mix, through Step 1, in a pitcher. Carefully pour the mixture into ice cube trays and freeze. The coffee ice cubes keep the milk punch chilled without diluting it.

Bacon Waffles with Pecan Chicken Tenders

HANDS-ON **1 HOUR, 25 MINUTES** TOTAL **1 HOUR, 25 MINUTES,**
INCLUDING PECAN CHICKEN TENDERS SERVES **8**

As far as I am concerned, you could wrap bacon around a stick and it would be good. Waffles alone . . . amazing. Waffles with bacon . . . stop it!

2 cups (8 ½ ounces) all-purpose flour

2 tablespoons granulated sugar

1 tablespoon baking powder

½ teaspoon kosher salt

5 bacon slices, cooked and crumbled

1 ¼ cups whole milk

¼ cup salted butter, melted

2 large eggs

Pecan Chicken Tenders (recipe follows)

16 wooden skewers or picks (optional)

Maple syrup

1 Preheat a waffle iron to medium-high. Whisk together the flour, sugar, baking powder, kosher salt, and bacon in a medium bowl. Stir in the milk, melted butter, and eggs.

2 Cook the batter, in batches, spooning ½ cup batter into each quadrant of the preheated, lightly greased waffle iron; cook waffles until lightly browned, 3 to 4 minutes.

3 Top each waffle with 1 chicken tender. Drizzle with maple syrup, and serve warm. (These may be skewered so they are easy to eat out of hand.)

Pecan Chicken Tenders

Vegetable oil

2 cups coarsely chopped pecans

2 cups (8 ½ ounces) all-purpose flour

1 cup (5 ¾ ounces) plain yellow cornmeal

½ cup chopped shallots

1 tablespoon kosher salt

1 tablespoon chopped fresh rosemary

1 teaspoon freshly ground black pepper

1 large egg

½ cup whole milk

16 chicken breast tenders

1 Pour the oil to a depth of 2 inches into a Dutch oven; heat over high to 325°F. Stir together the pecans, flour, cornmeal, shallots, salt, rosemary, and pepper in a shallow dish.

2 Whisk together the egg and milk in a shallow bowl. Dip the chicken tenders, 1 at a time, in the egg mixture; dredge in the pecan-flour mixture, pressing to adhere. Fry in batches 5 to 6 minutes or until done. Drain on a wire rack over paper towels. **Makes 16**

Sausage & Grits Quiches

HANDS-ON 35 MINUTES   TOTAL **1 HOUR, 30 MINUTES**   SERVES **8**

This recipe can be adapted from its petite size. Double the recipe and bake in a 13- x 9-inch baking dish for 1 hour. It also freezes beautifully, which are the most joyful four words in the English language if you love to throw parties.

1 (1-pound) package ground pork sausage

2 cups lower-sodium chicken broth

1 cup whipping cream

½ teaspoon table salt

1 cup uncooked regular grits

4 ounces Asiago cheese, grated
   (about 1 cup)

¼ teaspoon black pepper

4 ounces white Cheddar cheese,
   shredded (about 1 cup)

3 large eggs, lightly beaten

1 (10-ounce) package frozen chopped
   spinach, thawed and drained

1 ½ tablespoons plain white cornmeal

1 Cook the sausage in a large skillet over medium-high, stirring often, 5 minutes or until the sausage is no longer pink; remove from the skillet, and drain.

2 Preheat the oven to 350°F. Bring the broth, cream, and salt to a boil in a large saucepan over medium-high. Gradually whisk in the grits, and return to a boil.

3 Cover, reduce the heat to medium-low, and simmer, whisking occasionally, 12 to 15 minutes or until thickened. Remove from the heat; stir in the Asiago cheese, pepper, and ¾ cup of the Cheddar cheese until melted. (The mixture will be very thick.)

4 Gradually stir about one-fourth of the hot grits into the eggs; stir the egg mixture into the remaining hot grits. Stir in the spinach and sausage until blended.

5 Sprinkle the bottom and sides of 8 (6-ounce) lightly greased ramekins with cornmeal. Spoon the grits mixture evenly into the ramekins; sprinkle with the remaining Cheddar cheese.

6 Bake in the preheated oven for 25 minutes or until no longer jiggly in the center. Remove from the oven to a wire rack, and cool 30 minutes.

Note

To freeze: Prepare the recipe as directed through Step 5. Cover tightly with plastic wrap and heavy-duty aluminum foil. Place the quiches in ziplock plastic freezer bags. Freeze up to 1 month. Bake frozen quiche as directed in Step 6 until heated through.

Tantalizing Tea Tables and Trays

A tea can be as elegant as a formal reception to entertain a great number of people or as cozy as cinnamon toast before a fire with close friends. The secret is to brew a good pot, and set a tempting tray or table.

An afternoon tea at home is served by the hostess and is usually brought in from the kitchen already made. A bare tray (never use a covering for tea), is arranged to make serving easy for the hostess. The teapot is at hand in the lower right and a jug of hot water nearby for those who like their tea weakened. Grouped behind the pot are a small plate of lemon slices, a small pitcher of milk (not cream for a serious tea drinker), and a bowl of lump sugar to its left. If loose tea is used, a strainer and waste bowl may be included on the tray. The tea plates with napkins between each and butter knives placed with handles facing the guests are stacked in the upper left. Teacups with saucers and spoons to the right may be stacked in two's (but no more), if necessary. Hot buttered toast, cake, or other tea fare is brought in afterward and put on the table.

BRIDAL
TEA

BLUSHING MIMOSAS

SALMON-CUCUMBER
TEA SANDWICHES

CREAMED CHICKEN
IN BISCUIT BOWLS

LONG-STEMMED
STRAWBERRIES WITH
LEMON CURD DIP

CHOCOLATE
MOUSSE IN PASTRY
TART SHELLS

BRIDAL TEA

I love brides! I was in my aunt's wedding when I was six years old, and I thought she was the most beautiful person I had ever seen. Then Princess Diana got married and the deal was sealed. One of the best times of my life was when I planned my wedding and was a bride myself. I will tell anyone that it's the reason I cater. Since I was happy with Luke and couldn't get married every week, I decided that I needed to get into the business. Now I am as happy as a pig in mud. I am around brides all day every day. Their excitement and joy is infectious. I also think my love of brides is the reason I have hosted so many bridal teas.

The bridal tea is a lovely way to honor the bride without expecting guests to bring a gift like you would with a shower. Many times a bride or an engaged couple might have three or more showers, and usually the bridal party and close family members are invited to all of them. By the time the wedding comes around you have spent money on a wedding gift, shower gifts, clothes for the wedding weekend, and a bridesmaid's dress that you will never, and I mean never, wear again. It can be one hearty investment.

I would advise you to keep the menu light, and just because it's called a tea doesn't mean you can't include a crisp Champagne cocktail or a fruit-flavored vodka drink. A tea punch is also a great libation option.

Blushing Mimosas

HANDS-ON **5 MINUTES**   TOTAL **5 MINUTES**   SERVES **8**

There is hardly a better way to start a party than with a fluted glass filled with bubbly. I love mimosas, but they have become a bit trite. A splash of pineapple and grenadine is the perfect shot in the arm for this tired classic.

2 cups orange juice, chilled

1 cup pineapple juice, chilled

2 tablespoons grenadine

1 (750-milliliter) bottle sparkling wine or Champagne, chilled*

Assorted citrus wheels (optional)

Maraschino cherries (optional)

1 Stir together the orange juice, pineapple juice, and grenadine in a pitcher. Set the pitcher in an ice-filled tray to keep chilled.

2 Pour equal parts of the orange juice mixture and sparkling wine into Champagne flutes. Garnish with a citrus wheel or maraschino cherry, if desired. Serve immediately.

Note

*2 (12-ounce) cans ginger ale or lemon-lime soda may be substituted for the sparkling wine.

Write a Charming Thank-You Note

Whether you received a hostess gift for hosting or are the bride who was showered with everything on your registry list, knowing the ins and outs of a proper thank-you note is a key to Southern charm.

THE 5 KEY ELEMENTS OF EVERY SOUTHERN THANK-YOU NOTE

1 START WITH THE DATE AND SALUTATION

Send your note, written in black ink, within a week of receiving a gift.

2 SAY THANKS RIGHT OFF THE BAT

Be specific about why you are writing the note. If you're thanking someone for a monetary gift, refer to their "generosity" rather than mentioning the amount.

3 COMPLIMENT THE KIND GESTURE

Don't be afraid to go over the top—everyone loves an effusive compliment, as long as it's heartfelt.

4 ALLUDE TO THE FUTURE

Anticipate another get-together, or if you're writing about a gift, be sure to tell them how you plan to use it.

5 FINISH WITH SINCERE REGARDS

Reiterate your gratitude, then close the letter on an intimate note, signing your first and last name. Don't forget to proofread before you postmark!

64

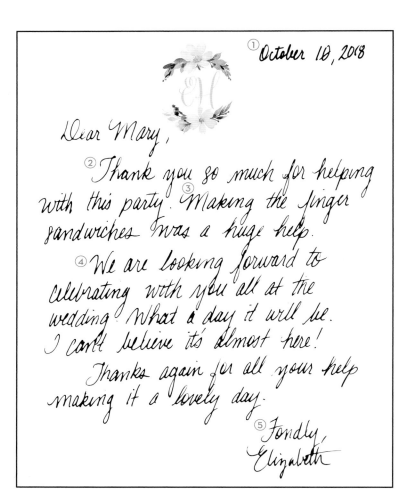

① October 10, 2018

Dear Mary,

② Thank you so much for helping with this party. ③ Making the finger sandwiches was a huge help.

④ We are looking forward to celebrating with you all at the wedding. What a day it will be. I can't believe it's almost here!

Thanks again for all your help making it a lovely day.

⑤ Fondly,
Elizabeth

Salmon-Cucumber Tea Sandwiches

(photograph on page 60)

HANDS-ON **15 MINUTES**   TOTAL **30 MINUTES**   SERVES **8**

Tea sandwiches are lovely because they can be made ahead of time. This combination of smoked salmon and cucumber is heavenly. I have never met someone who would turn down a tea sandwich. After all, they are so small and dainty, most people think they are void of calories altogether.

1 (8-ounce) package cream cheese, softened

3 tablespoons fresh lemon juice (from 1 lemon)

3 teaspoons grated white onion

½ teaspoon kosher salt

16 thin sandwich bread slices

1 medium English cucumber

4 ounces sliced smoked salmon

Fresh dill

1 Stir together the cream cheese, lemon juice, onion, and salt until well blended. Spread about 1 tablespoon onto each bread slice.

2 Cut the cucumber into thin rounds. Cut the rounds into half-moons. Divide the cucumbers and smoked salmon among the prepared bread slices. Gently press to adhere. Sprinkle with the fresh dill to taste.

3 Cover with plastic wrap, and chill 15 minutes to 12 hours. Trim the crusts from the chilled slices, and cut each slice into 2 triangles. Serve open-face or sandwich the triangles together, as desired.

Creamed Chicken in Biscuit Bowls

HANDS-ON **30 MINUTES**   TOTAL **1 HOUR, INCLUDING BISCUIT BOWLS**   SERVES **8**

I believe in homemade biscuits. I also believe that getting ready for a party in your home can be overwhelming. There are dust bunnies to catch, pillows to fluff, and children with dirty hands to yell at. Sometimes we need a shortcut, and this, my friends, is it.

2 tablespoons (1 ounce) salted butter
½ cup finely chopped onion (about 1 small onion)
½ cup finely chopped celery
½ cup sliced fresh mushrooms
1 (10 ¾-ounce) can condensed cream of chicken soup
½ cup whole milk
¼ teaspoon dried tarragon
4 ounces sharp Cheddar cheese, shredded (about 1 cup)

2 ½ cups chopped cooked chicken
½ (16-ounce) package frozen peas and carrots, thawed
1 (2-ounce) jar diced pimientos, drained
¼ teaspoon table salt
½ teaspoon black pepper
Biscuit Bowls (recipe follows)
Chopped fresh parsley (optional)

1 Melt the butter in a large skillet over medium-high; add the onion, celery, and mushrooms, and sauté 2 to 3 minutes or until tender.

2 Whisk in the soup, milk, and tarragon; cook over medium-low 3 minutes, stirring occasionally. Add the cheese, stirring until melted. Stir in the cooked chicken, peas and carrots, diced pimiento, salt, and pepper. Cook over low, stirring often, 10 minutes or until thoroughly heated. Spoon the warm chicken mixture evenly into the Biscuit Bowls. Garnish with the chopped fresh parsley, if desired.

Biscuit Bowls

1 (16.3-ounce) can refrigerated jumbo flaky biscuits

1 Preheat the oven to 350°F. Roll each biscuit into a 5-inch circle. Invert 8 (6-ounce) ramekins, several inches apart, on a lightly greased baking sheet. Lightly grease the outside of the cups.

2 Mold the flattened biscuits around the ramekins. Bake in the preheated oven for 14 minutes. Remove; cool. Gently remove the biscuit bowls from the cups. **Makes 8**

Long-Stemmed Strawberries with Lemon Curd Dip

HANDS-ON **10 MINUTES**   TOTAL **10 MINUTES**   SERVES **8**

Long-stemmed strawberries are likely few and far between at your local grocery store. Find a local farmer and order strawberries cut with long stems during the spring when they are at their peak. I know it seems like a lot of sugar for a dime, but it's the subtle details that your guests will never forget.

My grandmother made this exact recipe for my cousin Alexander's christening. All the children had been relegated to my grandmother's bedroom. I knew good and well that I wasn't allowed to eat in my grandmother's room. I hid three strawberries in the pocket of my dress and completely forgot about them until I sat on my grandmother's bed. They squished into her silk bedspread and my lace dress. I tearfully told mom what happened, and she and a friend furiously worked to get the stains out of the bedspread. Finally, by some miracle, the stain came out. They decided to toast their success with Champagne while they used a blow dryer to dry the wet spot. They were talking, laughing, and sipping and completely forgot about the work at hand, and all of the sudden the spread caught on fire. Champagne flutes were turned upside down to douse the fire. There was no getting out of it now. My grandmother had to be informed. I would imagine that this is what someone feels like right before they face a firing squad. Mama finally got up the nerve to tell her. My grandmother laughed and explained that it was her second bedspread. She said that she never put her good spreads out during parties for fear that something like this might happen. The party lesson here is that if you have something you truly treasure, put it up during your party or your punch-drunk children might set it on fire.

½ (8-ounce) package cream cheese, softened

½ cup lemon curd (such as Stonewall Kitchen)

½ teaspoon lemon zest, plus more for garnish (from 1 lemon)

¼ cup heavy cream

24 fresh long-stemmed strawberries

1 Beat the cream cheese, lemon curd, and ¼ teaspoon of lemon zest with an electric mixer at medium speed until smooth, about 2 minutes. In a separate bowl, beat the heavy cream with a mixer at high speed until soft peaks form, about 2 minutes.

2 Gently fold the whipped cream into the cream cheese mixture. Chill until ready to serve. Garnish with the lemon zest, and serve with the strawberries.

Chocolate Mousse in Pastry Tart Shells

HANDS-ON **45 MINUTES**   TOTAL **4 HOURS, 50 MINUTES,**
INCLUDING TART SHELLS   SERVES **8**

Triple the tart shell recipe and freeze the extra so you're always party ready. You never know when you'll need it, but it is good to know you have it. Now, that's insurance I understand.

1 (12-ounce) package semisweet
   chocolate chips
2 ½ cups whipping cream
1 teaspoon vanilla extract

1 tablespoon rum
Pastry Tart Shells (recipe follows)
Sweetened whipped cream
Grated chocolate

1   Microwave the chocolate chips and ½ cup of the cream in a small glass bowl at HIGH 1 ½ minutes or until melted. Stir in the vanilla and rum, blending well. Cool 5 minutes.

2   Whip the remaining 2 cups of cream with an electric mixer at medium speed, and fold into the chocolate mixture. Fill the tart shells with the mousse. Garnish with the sweetened cream and grated chocolate. Chill 2 hours.

Pastry Tart Shells

2 cups (8 ½ ounces) all-purpose flour
1 teaspoon table salt

⅔ cup cold vegetable shortening,
   cut into pieces
6 tablespoons ice water
¼ cup (2 ounces) butter, softened

1   Stir together the flour and salt in a medium bowl; cut in the shortening with a pastry blender until mixture resembles coarse meal. Cover and chill 30 minutes.

2   Preheat the oven to 425°F. Add the ice water, a bit at a time, to the flour mixture, stirring just until the dry ingredients are moistened. Shape the dough into 2 balls.

3   Roll a dough ball out on a floured surface to ¼-inch thickness (about a 9-inch circle); spread with 2 tablespoons of the butter. Fold the dough into thirds; roll again to ¼-inch thickness. Cut into 4 (5-inch) rounds. Repeat with the remaining dough ball.

4   Invert a 12-cup muffin pan. Mold the dough over 8 cups, and prick with a fork. Bake in the preheated oven for 10 to 12 minutes. Remove and cool on the pan 2 minutes. Gently lift the shells from the pan and cool completeley, about 10 minutes. **Makes 8**

Come by for a Drink, Y'all

Out of all the types of parties to throw, this is the easiest one to host. When you send an invitation to people to come by for a drink, your guests don't expect much. My MeMa used to get so fed up when people invited her over for a drink and would put out only a bowl of nuts. But honestly, you hardly have to do more than a bowl of nuts. So with the bar set that low, honey, this is your time to shine. Gild that lily!

bubbles & BIRDS

Chilled Champagne

Mama's Fried Chicken   Black-Eyed Pea Cakes

Smoked Catfish Dip
with Pork Rinds

BUBBLES AND BIRDS

Since I'm from the Mississippi Delta, my whole life has been big. . . .

We have big weddings and big fish fries. We have big debutante balls and big backyard barbecues. Celebrating the fancy and the no-fuss is a way of life in the Delta, but no matter what, we always go big or go home. Football game days in Oxford are a perfect example. It is common for chandeliers and candelabras to appear in our tailgate tents, proving that pregame in the Delta is no back-of-the-pickup affair. For parties at our house growing up, Mama loved to mix her antique sterling silver with her rustic McCarty pottery from Merigold, Mississippi. These high-low contrasts give the Delta character.

I think that is why I'm so fond of this bubbles and birds party. People love the unexpected: It's memorable. Think about it like this: You get dressed up for a lovely party, and they serve beef tenderloin, rolls, and horseradish mayonnaise. The centerpieces are lovely glass bowls filled with hydrangeas and roses. Fifteen round tables with gold chairs and ivory satin tablecloths surround the room. When you leave and call your mama on the way home from the party, you have very little to say except that it was lovely. I am sure it was. But let's say you get dressed up, you go to a party, and they have nothing but fried chicken and free-flowing Champagne, burlap and silk tablecloths, and some farm tables with a few gold chairs mixed in. There are beautiful arrangements on the table filled with greenery and garland. You could talk to your mama about this all night long. People take notice when things are a little off-kilter. Parties like this one leave a lasting impression on people, and that is what it is all about.

Champagne Primer

Sparkling wine and Champagne are often confused. True Champagne (note the capital "C") is produced in the region of the same name in France. It is often quite expensive. If the label says "champagne" (lowercase "c") but it is not from France, you can rest assured you are not getting the real deal. Don't fret, there are sparkling and delicious alternatives available from producers around the globe.

PRODUCTION METHODS

CLASSIC METHOD (MÉTHODE CLASSIQUE) Still wine is fermented first in a barrel. A second fermentation of the wine happens in the bottle when yeast, nutrients, and a sugar are added and the bottles are sealed and aged. Carbon dioxide is released as the wine ferments and is captured in the bottle.

CHARMAT METHOD Fermentation of still white wine happens in a pressurized, stainless-steel tank and then yeast and sugar are added. When the sugar converts to alcohol, the wine is filtered and bottled. This is the most widely used method for sparkling wines produced in the U.S.

LABEL LINGO

BLANC DE BLANC white Champagne made from white grapes

BLANC DE NOIR white Champagne made from red grapes

BRUT NATUREL bone-dry with no sugar added

EXTRA BRUT very dry

BRUT dry to semisweet

SEC semisweet

DEMISEC sweet

KNOW YOUR BUBBLES

ASTI Sweet sparkling white wine made from a single tank fermentation of Moscato Bianco (Muscat) grapes in the Italian Piedmont region near the towns of Asti and Alba. Serve chilled with fruit, pastries, and simple desserts.

CALIFORNIA SPARKLING WINE Over 300 producers in the state make sparkling wine, from dry to sweet, primarily made from Chardonnay, Pinot Blanc, and Pinot Noir grapes. Most use the Charmat method. Serve for brunch and festive celebrations.

CAVA Dry to sweet white or rosé sparkling wine produced most commonly in Catalonia, Spain, from Parellada, Xarello, or Macebeu grapes using the classic method. Serve with crudité, cheese, creamy sauces, salads, and seafood.

CREMANT Aged, sparkling French white and rosé wines made outside the region of Champagne from hand-picked grapes using the classic method. Serve with omelets and rich foods, but also salads and pizza.

FRANCIACORTA Dry to sweet sparkling white and red wines made from Chardonnay, Pinot Nero, and Pinot Bianco grapes in the province of Brescia (Lombardy) in Italy using the classic method. Serve with ravioli, truffles, and (drier varieties) with tomato sauce and pizza.

LAMBRUSCO A red wine grape and type of red wine made in the Emilia-Romagna and Lombardy regions of Italy. From dry to sweet, Lambrusco is mostly made using the Charmat method. Slightly sparkling "frizzante" Lambrusco is the most prized. Serve with sausages, cured meats, barbecue, aged dry cheeses, pizza, peaches, and nectarines.

PROSECCO Light, sparkling white wine named for the village of Prosecco, where it originated. It is traditionally made from Glera grapes using the Charmat method, but other varieties may also be used. Serve with nuts, charcuterie, fried and salty foods, and seafood.

Mama's Fried Chicken

HANDS-ON **1 HOUR, 5 MINUTES**   TOTAL **3 HOURS, 5 MINUTES**   SERVES **8 TO 10**

There isn't a better way to start a party than to greet guests at the door with a silver tray filled with ice-cold Champagne. The party mood is instantly set. The stress from a tough day or even a fuss with your spouse on the way over instantly dissolves.

2 (3- to 4-pound) whole chickens,
   cut into pieces
2 teaspoons table salt
2 teaspoons black pepper

4 cups whole buttermilk
Self-rising flour
Vegetable oil
Hot sauce (optional)

1 Sprinkle the chickens evenly with the salt and pepper. Place each chicken in a shallow dish or large ziplock plastic bag, and add 2 cups of buttermilk to each dish or bag. Cover or seal, and chill at least 2 hours.

2 Remove the chickens from the buttermilk, discarding the buttermilk. Dredge the chicken in the flour.

3 Pour the oil to a depth of 1 ½ inches in a deep skillet or Dutch oven; heat to 360°F. Add half of the chicken, a few pieces at a time, and then cover and cook 6 minutes.

4 Uncover the chicken, and cook 9 minutes. Turn the chicken; cover and cook 6 minutes. Uncover and cook 5 to 9 minutes, turning the chicken the last 3 minutes for even browning, if necessary. Drain on paper towels. Repeat the process with the remaining chicken. Serve warm with the hot sauce, if desired.

Cocktail Parties and Cocktail Suppers

The cocktail party is possibly the easiest and most misunderstood way to entertain a large group of people. The party may begin anywhere from 5 o'clock on, and the invitation may or may not state the hour. If the guest list is large, groups may be invited for a two hour period, but don't be surprised if a few guests have such a good time that they stay through the first list and mingle with the second group of guests.

Guests are given a choice of food, the hors d'oeuvres may be placed on one table, or at several vantage points for better serving of guests. Since guests usually have to stand at cocktail parties, pick-up foods are served. It's wise to have a choice of these tidbits, and be sure to have plenty of each kind.

A cocktail supper is usually held for a specific group; guests at a wedding reception, or for friends who are going to a concert afterwards. Hot foods are often served from chafing dishes at this type party, and in addition to these hot foods the hostess may serve the usual dips and open-face sandwiches.

In both type entertainments the bar, serving both alcoholic and non-alcoholic beverages, should be set apart from the table serving the hors d'oeuvres.

Black-Eyed Pea Cakes

(photograph on page 79)

HANDS-ON **30 MINUTES**   TOTAL **1 HOUR, 30 MINUTES**   SERVES **15**

I have a huge affection for peas. When I was growing up, we would often have a huge lunch that rivaled any "meat and three" restaurant. We had at least four vegetables from the farm, and black-eyed peas and cornbread were staples. I loved to eat my peas with ketchup, which is strange but true. I love to serve this pea cake with a sweet tomato relish for a nod to my childhood days.

1 small onion, chopped

Olive oil

2 (15.5-ounce) cans black-eyed peas, drained and rinsed

1 (8-ounce) container chive-and-onion cream cheese, softened

1 large egg

½ teaspoon table salt

1 teaspoon hot sauce

1 (8-ounce) package hush puppy mix with onion

Sour cream

Green Tomato Relish (page 284)

1 Sauté the onion in 1 tablespoon hot oil in a large skillet over medium-high until tender.

2 Process the onion, 1 can of peas, cream cheese, egg, salt, and hot sauce in a blender or food processor until the mixture is smooth, stopping to scrape down the sides. Stir in the hush puppy mix, and gently fold in the remaining can of peas.

3 Shape the mixture by 2 tablespoonfuls into 3-inch patties, and place on a wax paper-lined baking sheet. Cover and chill 1 hour.

4 Cook the patties, in batches, in 3 tablespoons hot oil, adding oil as needed, in a large skillet over medium for 1 ½ minutes on each side or until the patties are golden brown. Drain the patties on paper towels, and keep warm. Serve with sour cream and green tomato relish.

Smoked Catfish Dip
with Pork Rinds

HANDS-ON **10 MINUTES**   TOTAL **1 HOUR, 30 MINUTES**   SERVES **36**

This award-winning dip was made famous by The Crown Restaurant in Indianola, Mississippi, and is always served with Bremner wafers. I was completely obsessed from my very first bite.

5 (8-ounce) skinless catfish fillets

**1 ½ (8-ounce) packages cream
   cheese, softened**

**2 teaspoons Creole seasoning
   (such as Tony Chachere's)**

¼ teaspoon hickory liquid smoke

**⅛ teaspoon hot sauce
   (such as Tabasco)**

Paprika (optional)

Pork rinds

1 Preheat the broiler with the oven rack 3 inches from the heat. Place the catfish on a baking sheet lined with aluminum foil; broil until the fish is browned and flakes with a fork, about 6 to 7 minutes. Cool completely, about 15 minutes; use a fork to flake apart.

2 Beat the cream cheese, Creole seasoning, liquid smoke, and hot sauce with an electric mixer at medium speed until well blended. Add the catfish; beat at low just until the catfish is incorporated, leaving the catfish in small pieces for texture. Cover and chill 1 hour. Sprinkle with paprika just before serving, if desired. Serve with the pork rinds.

PARTY RULE NO. 4

Make guests feel special and at home

*A high-low snack at the ready the moment guests arrive sets the tone.
A glass of Champagne says, "Your presence is a special occasion."
Pairing it with pork rinds says, "Put your feet up and stay awhile."*

SUNDOWN ON
THE GROUNDS

Bourbon
Rickey

Candied
Bacon Grissini

Smoky Spiced
Pecans

Crunchy
Cheese Coins

SUNDOWN ON THE GROUNDS

MENU FOR 12

Merigold, Mississippi, is famous for McCarty Pottery. Lee and Pup McCarty started their pottery business in the 1960s, but it was more than just a business—it was a culture and a lifestyle. Their home has been featured in many magazines, and their parties were legendary.

One party that people would die to be invited to was a Sundown. This was an impromptu party held on the front porch of their home. Lee and Pup greeted guests upon arrival with a McCarty tumbler filled with gin and tonic. Guests chatted as they sipped and nibbled on passed hors d'oeuvres. As soon as the sun started to descend, as if on cue, everyone turned to watch in silence. Once the sun had set and night fell, everyone went inside and the real ruckus began. It was Lee and Pup's way of celebrating something that happened 365 days a year, but that we hardly took the time to notice.

Sunsets are magnificent in the Mississippi Delta. The land is so flat that it looks like the sun hits a puddle on the ground and then disappears. The idea of finding something ordinary to celebrate is a wonderful way to remind people]to stop and smell the roses. These parties don't require a ton of effort. Set out a good selection of booze or wine and some tiny bites. The whole point is to stop and notice the good that is all around us.

Bourbon Rickey

HANDS-ON **5 MINUTES**   TOTAL **5 MINUTES**   SERVES **12**

Normally this classic cocktail is made with gin. We decided to change it up a little by replacing the gin with bourbon. In the fall, try adding a little maple syrup for even more flavor.

3 cups fresh lime juice (from 6 to 8 limes)

3 cups (24 ounces) bourbon

¼ cup simple syrup

Ice

3 cups club soda, chilled

12 lime wedges (optional)

Mint sprigs (optional)

Divide the lime juice, bourbon, and simple syrup evenly among 12 Collins glasses. Add the ice to glasses, and top off each with ¼ cup club soda. Garnish each glass with a lime wedge and mint sprig, if desired.

Note

Most any cocktail can be respun into
a refreshing mocktail. Swap the bourbon and
club soda in this one with cola and garnish.
It's hard to beat a refreshing Lime Coke.

Setting the Scene

BRING THE INDOORS OUT

Up the ante on the usual drinks station by creating an outdoor, walk-up bar—outfitted with pretty indoor accents—that allows easy access to refills.

A "candelier" hung from a tree over a seating area or table adds a dose of drama to the outdoors. Cafe or bistro lights can also turn your backyard into a glamorous, twinkling venue.

Choose flowers in sunset hues to match this party theme and arrange them so they have an easy, garden-fresh feel, even if you just picked them up from the supermarket. Big, bold dahlias and roses mix beautifully with magnolia leaves and woodsy rosemary sprigs.

Smoky Spiced Pecans

(photograph on page 87)

HANDS-ON **10 MINUTES**   TOTAL **1 HOUR**   SERVES **12**

So many recipes that look seemingly easy on paper can be the most challenging. Toasted pecans are one of my favorite sit-around hors d'oeuvres but they make me crazy. I have burned as many batches as I have had success with them. I am easily distracted and tend to put them in the oven and then wander off. The smell of burning nuts always snaps me back to attention. When you make these, stay in the kitchen.

3 cups water

6 tablespoons maple syrup

3 cups pecan halves

1 teaspoon kosher salt

2 teaspoons smoked paprika

¼ teaspoon cayenne pepper

1 Preheat the oven to 350°F. Bring 3 cups water and the maple syrup just to a boil in a medium saucepan over high ; add the pecan halves and remove from the heat. Let stand 15 minutes; drain.

2 Stir together the salt, smoked paprika, and cayenne pepper in a medium bowl; add the pecans, tossing to coat. Spread in a single layer on a lightly greased 15- x 10-inch rimmed baking sheet. Bake in the preheated oven for 15 minutes or until lightly toasted, stirring once.

3 Cool on the pan 20 minutes. Store in an airtight container up to 2 weeks. (These also make tasty favors for parting guests. Just fill a small cellophane gift bag, and tie with a ribbon or twine with a "thank-you for coming!" tag attached.)

Candied Bacon Grissini

HANDS-ON **10 MINUTES**   TOTAL **1 HOUR**   SERVES **10 TO 12**

Candied bacon, or "pig candy" as we often call it, is always a home run. We love to keep the bacon strips whole and stuff them into a mint julep cup to make the perfect nibble on any bar. They're like magic pig wands when they're wrapped around a breadstick.

1 cup packed dark brown sugar

1 (16-ounce) package thick bacon slices

1 (3-ounce) package grissini

1 Preheat the oven to 350°F. Spread the brown sugar evenly on a plate, and set aside while you wrap the grissini.

2 Wrap 1 bacon slice around each grissini, starting at 1 end, and barely overlapping to cover the entire stick. Roll each wrapped grissini in the brown sugar to lightly coat the bacon.

3 Arrange the wrapped grissini in a single layer on 2 lightly greased wire racks in 2 aluminum foil-lined broiler pans. Bake in the preheated oven for 30 to 45 minutes or until done. Cool completely, about 20 minutes.

Crunchy Cheese Coins

HANDS-ON **25 MINUTES**   TOTAL **40 MINUTES**   SERVES **24**

Yes, you read this recipe right! It has rice cereal in it. I cannot imagine a more unexpected ingredient unless we called for sardines. The rice cereal adds a delightful crunch that your guests will never suspect. Snap . . . crackle . . . pop, anyone?

1 cup (about 4 ¼ ounces) all-purpose flour

4 ounces sharp Cheddar cheese, shredded (about 1 cup)

½ cup (4 ounces) salted butter, softened

½ teaspoon Worcestershire sauce

½ teaspoon kosher salt

¼ teaspoon hot sauce (such as Tabasco)

1 cup crisp rice cereal (such as Rice Krispies)

1 Preheat the oven to 350°F. Combine the flour, cheese, butter, Worcestershire, salt, and hot sauce in a food processor, and process until incorporated.

2 Transfer the mixture to a large bowl; stir in the rice cereal with a spoon, pressing the mixture into the sides of bowl until well combined. Pinch off pieces about the size of a nickel.

3 Place the cheese "coins" on an ungreased baking sheet; press each coin with a fork. Bake in the preheated oven until slightly golden around the edges, about 12 minutes.

SEAN MINOR

2016
SAUVIGNON BLANC

Summer Nights

Frozen Watermelon Mojito

Heirloom Tomato & Avocado
Salad with Blue Corn Chips

Wonder Wings with Cider-
Vinegar-Brown Butter Drizzle

Individual Red, White,
& Blue Trifles

SUMMER NIGHTS

They say that people who have front porches are generally happier people. I don't know who "they" are, but I probably heard it on the TODAY show since it's my only news source. This tidbit really caught my attention, and it made me wonder if I was happier in my past houses that had porches than the ones that didn't. This brought me back to all of the parties I had on those porches, and a smile came over my face as I remembered each and every party. I remember the crawfish boils Luke and I had at his house on Alexander Street when we were dating; the days when friends and neighbors walked over for a beer on our porch; the Easters that we spent drinking mimosas and watching the girls hunt for Easter eggs from our porch in the Rosedale house; and the times at the Hillcrest house when we talked around the porch fireplace late into the night. All of these parties were poorly planned and thrown together at the last minute, and some weren't planned at all. In fact, I find that those are always the best parties.

The Fourth of July in Mississippi is hot, and I mean as hot as the hinges of hell. Most people escape to the lakes, beaches, or mountains for relief. During the past years I've had large weddings that weekend so we stayed home. Oxford has a wonderful celebration that starts with a bike parade around the square and ends with fireworks at the baseball stadium that rivals any big city's show. That afternoon is the perfect time for a relaxed porch party. Make sure you have plenty of iced-down drinks for both the big and little kids. We always have plenty of Mason jars with holes poked in the lids for the kids to catch lightening bugs. Glow stick necklaces and wands are also a fun addition. There is nothing like a little neon bling to take your porch party to another level. Once the sun goes down, spread blankets out on the lawn and turn up the patriotic tunes. My friend Stephanie and I play "Proud to Be an American" on repeat and sing at the top of our lungs with tears running down our faces until someone takes over the playlist and demands that we don't touch it again. There is nothing like watching the fireworks show on the front porch.

Frozen Watermelon Mojito

HANDS-ON **10 MINUTES**   TOTAL **2 HOURS, 10 MINUTES**   SERVES **8**

Watermelon has never been my favorite. There I said it! I have always been ashamed to admit it. I feel like it makes me less of an American. But I sure did change my mind after drinking this refreshing frozen concoction. Honey, I was humming "Yankee Doodle Dandy" after my third one!

5 cups seeded and cubed watermelon

½ cup granulated sugar

½ cup water

2 mint sprigs, plus more for garnish

¾ cup (6 ounces) white rum

½ cup fresh lime juice (from 4 to 6 limes)

1 cup club soda, chilled

Very small watermelon wedges

Lime wedges

1 Place the watermelon cubes in a single layer on a baking sheet, and freeze until solid, about 2 hours.

2 While the watermelon freezes, bring the sugar and ¼ cup water to a boil in a small saucepan over medium-high. Add the mint sprigs, reduce the heat to low, and simmer 5 minutes. Remove the syrup from the heat, and let cool 30 minutes. Remove and discard the mint sprigs. Chill until cooled, at least 30 minutes.

3 Combine the frozen watermelon, mint syrup, rum, and lime juice in a blender; process until smooth, 8 to 10 seconds. Stir in the club soda. Divide the mixture evenly among 8 glasses. Garnish each with a watermelon wedge, lime wedge, and mint sprig, if desired.

Summer
nights

Frozen Watermelon Mojito

Heirloom Tomato & Avocado
Salad with Blue Corn Chips

Wonder Wings with Cider-
Vinegar-Brown Butter Drizzle

Individual Red, White,
& Blue Trifles

Heirloom Tomato and Avocado Salsa with Blue Corn Chips

HANDS-ON **20 MINUTES**   TOTAL **20 MINUTES**   SERVES **8**

When searching for heirloom tomatoes, try to find them in as many colors as you can. Avocado and tomato salsa has become a party mainstay, but adding beautiful heirloom tomatoes will make this salsa the hit of the party. Blue corn chips are also a game changer. Serve jarred salsa with blue corn chips and people will think you did something special. If you really want to impress your guests, mix some classic corn chips with the blue corn chips. Now you have a showstopper on your hands.

1 ½ pounds heirloom tomatoes, small diced (about 3 ¼ cups)

¾ cup finely chopped red onion (from 1 small onion)

2 ripe avocados, peeled, pitted, and diced (about 2 cups)

1 jalapeño chile, seeded and finely chopped (about 3 tablespoons)

½ cup chopped fresh cilantro

¼ cup fresh lime juice (from 2 limes)

2 tablespoons olive oil

1 ½ teaspoons kosher salt

½ teaspoon ground cumin

¼ teaspoon black pepper

Cilantro leaves (optional)

Blue corn tortilla chips

Gently toss together the tomatoes, red onion, avocados, jalapeño, chopped cilantro, lime juice, olive oil, salt, cumin, and black pepper in a medium bowl. Garnish with the cilantro leaves, if desired. Serve with the tortilla chips.

Wonder Wings with Cider Vinegar-Brown Butter Drizzle

HANDS-ON **35 MINUTES**   TOTAL **1 HOUR, 15 MINUTES, INCLUDING DRIZZLE**   SERVES **8**

Drizzle is a relative term. When I make this recipe, I do a dainty drizzle and then just slather the heck out of it. This drizzle needs to be a slather.

3 pounds chicken wings

2 teaspoons vegetable oil

1 teaspoon kosher salt

½ teaspoon freshly ground
   black pepper

Cider Vinegar-Brown Butter-
   Honey Drizzle (recipe follows)

1 Preheat a gas grill to medium (350°F to 400°F) on 1 side, or push hot coals to 1 side of a charcoal grill. Dry each wing well with paper towels. Toss together the wings and oil in a large bowl. Sprinkle with the salt and pepper, and toss to coat.

2 Place the wings on oiled grates over the unlit side of the grill. Grill, covered with the grill lid, 15 minutes on each side. Transfer the chicken to the lit side of grill, and grill, uncovered, 10 to 12 minutes or until the skin is crispy and lightly charred, turning every 2 to 3 minutes. Toss the wings immediately with ¾ cup of the Cider Vinegar-Brown Butter-Honey Drizzle.

3 Let stand, tossing occasionally, 5 minutes before serving. Arrange the wings on a platter with a bowl of the remaining ¾ cup Cider Vinegar-Brown Butter-Honey Drizzle (and lots of napkins!) to serve.

Cider Vinegar-Brown Butter Drizzle

½ cup (4 ounces) salted butter

1 cup honey

2 tablespoons apple cider vinegar

1 Heat the butter in a saucepan over medium-high 5 minutes or until browned and fragrant. Transfer to a small bowl, and cool 5 minutes.

2 Heat the honey and vinegar in a saucepan over medium, stirring often, 2 minutes or until thoroughly heated. Whisk in the browned butter.
Makes 1 ½ cups

Individual Red, White & Blue Trifles

HANDS-ON **20 MINUTES**   TOTAL **40 MINUTES**   SERVES **8**

This dessert is very impressive and couldn't be any easier to make. It really is all about the assembly. Be patient and remember to keep the best-looking fruit closest to the glass so that the layers turn out beautifully. I especially love using a stemless martini or wineglass to serve the petite trifles.

1 (3.4-ounce) package vanilla instant pudding mix

2 cups whole milk

½ cup plain whole-milk Greek yogurt

1 ½ cups sliced fresh strawberries

2 tablespoons granulated sugar

½ cup heavy cream

1 tablespoon powdered sugar

1 (16-ounce) pound cake, cut into ¾-inch cubes (about 6 ½ cups)

1 ¼ cups fresh blueberries, plus more for garnish

2 medium-size ripe bananas, sliced

Mint sprigs (optional)

1   Whisk together the pudding mix, milk, and yogurt in a medium bowl until thickened, about 5 minutes. Cover and chill until ready to use.

2   Toss together the sliced strawberries and granulated sugar until the berries are coated. Let stand until juicy, 10 to 15 minutes.

3   Meanwhile, beat the heavy cream and powdered sugar with an electric mixer at high speed until stiff peaks form.

4   Place ¼ cup of the cake cubes in the bottom of each of 8 (12- to 16-ounce) glasses or Mason jars. Top each evenly with a layer of blueberries, about 2 tablespoons pudding, and another ¼ cup of cake cubes. Top each evenly with a layer of bananas, about 2 tablespoons pudding, and another ¼ cup of cake cubes. Top each with the strawberries and accumulated juices. Dollop with the whipped cream, and garnish the tops with additional blueberries and a mint sprig, if desired.

JOY
to the
GIRLS

Fancy Jigglers
Pimiento Cheese Rolls
Blue Cheese-Bacon Dip
Prosciutto-Wrapped
Asparagus with Citrus Drizzle
Mint Chocolate Truffles
Snowballs

JOY TO THE GIRLS

Julie Yoste, who is infamous for just being damn adorable, came up with the name for this party. You might remember her from the Yoste Roast recipe in my last cookbook, *What Can I Bring?* or my TODAY show segment where I explained that whether you've had a death in the family, are sick, or just have an ingrown toenail, Julie will appear with a magnum of wine and her roast and won't leave until they're both gone.

Thank God Julie has an amazing sense of humor and didn't kill me when I saw her at Sonic after that segment aired. But I always give credit where credit is due, unlike Lucius Lamar, (not my Luke . . . the other Lucius in town) who stole my friend Kara's cranberry salsa recipe and put it in *Bon Appétit* magazine. She still loves him but will never forgive or forget. When questioned about the incident Lucius replied: "Um, well that is true. However, I prefer creatively borrowed. Stole sounds so pedestrian, don't you think? It's not like I wore a ninja costume, broke into her secret cooking lair, and downloaded the recipe . . . or did I? Poor wronged Kara. I'll send her a potted plant."

What was I talking about . . . oh yes! . . . Julie and the Joy to the Girls. Well, Julie hosted this party for her daughter, Gigi, and her little girlfriends. They wore their pajamas and brought Christmas presents for animals at the local shelter. Julie made holiday treats for the girls, and they played Dirty Santa with the ornaments guests were asked to bring.

Now we tell our children to be kind to one another and not to take things that don't belong to them, but then promote this game that we know is going to make at least one child cry. Hell, I still get mad during this game. I will never forget the year a floozy from work stole a fluffy robe from me, and I got stuck with a dust buster. I wanted to cry my eyes out. Dirty Santa aside, the Joy to the Girls party was adorable and became a highlight of many holiday seasons.

Needless to say, I wanted to celebrate my girlfriends, so I stole Julie's Joy to the Girls party theme and began hosting an annual party for my closest friends. You know, the ones who make your heart leap a little when they send you a text message or you bump into them in the grocery. They're who you call when you need to be talked off that ledge and they're not afraid to ask who died when you ask for their tomato aspic recipe. You get the idea! This is a celebration of those you hold most dear to show how much you love and care for them.

Fancy Jigglers

HANDS-ON **10 MINUTES**   TOTAL **4 HOURS, 10 MINUTES,
INCLUDING 4 HOURS CHILLING**   SERVES **24**

*My great-grandmother was a congealed salad addict. Thank goodness she didn't know that
you could put booze in gelatin or she would have had to take a trip to Betty Ford. I cannot think
of a more fun way to start a party. Lord knows it makes me smile just thinking about it!*

½ cup cranberry juice

½ cup fresh grapefruit juice (from
   1 grapefruit)

¼ cup fresh lime juice (from 2 limes)

1 tablespoon agave nectar

3 (¼-ounce) envelopes unflavored gelatin

1 cup (8 ounces) tequila

½ cup (4 ounces) orange liqueur (such as
   Grand Marnier)

2 tablespoons edible gold leaf flecks

1 Stir together the cranberry juice, grapefruit juice, lime juice, and agave nectar in a
medium saucepan. Sprinkle the gelatin over the juices, and let stand until softened,
about 5 minutes. Place the pan over low, and cook, stirring constantly, until the
gelatin is dissolved, about 5 minutes. Remove from the heat, and stir in the tequila
and orange liqueur until combined.

2 Pour the mixture into a 9-inch square pan or silicone pan with individual square
molds.

3 Sprinkle the top with the edible gold leaf flecks. Chill until firm, about 4 hours,
or overnight. Cut into small squares or remove the squares from the molds, and
serve immediately.

Pimiento Cheese Rolls

HANDS-ON **25 MINUTES**   TOTAL **1 HOUR, 20 MINUTES, INCLUDING PIMIENTO CHEESE**
MAKES **1 DOZEN**

These savory puffs are so easy to make, yet so rich and impressive no one will know. Short on time? Just pick up a tub of your favorite pimiento cheese from the store. It'll be our secret!

1 (26.4-ounce) package frozen biscuits   **Pimiento Cheese (recipe follows)**
All-purpose flour

1 Arrange the frozen biscuits, with the sides touching, in 3 rows of 4 biscuits on a lightly floured surface. Let stand 30 to 45 minutes or until the biscuits are thawed but cool to the touch.

2 Preheat the oven to 375°F. Sprinkle the biscuits with flour. Press the edges together, and pat to form a 12- x 10-inch rectangle; spread evenly with the Pimiento Cheese.

3 Roll up, starting at 1 long end; cut into 12 (about 1-inch-thick) slices. Place 1 slice into each of 12 lightly greased 3-inch muffin pan cups.

4 Bake in the preheated oven for 20 to 25 minutes or until golden brown. Cool slightly, and remove from the pan.

HAM-AND-SWISS ROLLS: Omit the Pimiento Cheese. Stir together ¼ cup each of softened butter, brown mustard, and finely chopped sweet onion. Spread the mixture evenly over the 12- x 10-inch rectangle of the thawed dough; sprinkle evenly with 1 cup each of shredded Swiss cheese and chopped cooked ham. Proceed with the recipe as directed.

SAUSAGE-AND-CHEDDAR ROLLS: Omit the Pimiento Cheese. Spread ¼ cup softened butter evenly over the 12- x 10-inch rectangle of thawed dough; sprinkle evenly with 1 cup each of shredded Cheddar cheese and cooked, crumbled sausage. Proceed with the recipe as directed.

Pimiento Cheese

This is a classic recipe for pimiento cheese, but you know I believe in gilding the lily. For a twist, use shredded Muenster, white Cheddar, or smoked Gouda.

8 ounces sharp Cheddar cheese,   **1 (2-ounce) jar diced pimientos, drained**
  shredded (about 2 cups)   **1 teaspoon minced onion**
³/₄ cup mayonnaise   **¹/₄ teaspoon cayenne pepper**

Stir together all the ingredients in a medium bowl until mixed. Chill until ready to serve.   **Makes 2 cups**

Blue Cheese-Bacon Dip

(photograph on page 108)

HANDS-ON **20 MINUTES**   TOTAL **35 MINUTES**   SERVES **16**

Many people aren't huge fans of blue cheese. My friend Cordilla's husband Charlie cannot stand it. I served this dip at a Christmas party a few years ago, and I saw him holding court around this dip as he scooped cracker after cracker in it. After he had eaten his weight in it, I confessed to him that his new favorite dip was made of mountains of blue cheese. He didn't believe me, and to this day he still thinks I was joking.

By the way, adding a little crumbled bacon on top won't hurt anyone's feelings.

7 bacon slices, chopped

2 garlic cloves, minced

2 (8-ounce) packages cream cheese, softened

⅓ cup half-and-half

4 ounces crumbled blue cheese (about 1 cup)

2 tablespoons chopped fresh chives

3 tablespoons chopped walnuts, toasted

Grapes

Flatbread or assorted crackers

1 Preheat the oven to 350°F. Cook the bacon in a skillet over medium-high 10 minutes or until crisp. Remove the bacon from the skillet with a slotted spoon to drain on paper towels, reserving the drippings in the skillet. Add the garlic to the drippings in the skillet, and sauté 1 minute.

2 Beat the cream cheese with an electric mixer at medium speed until smooth. Add the half-and-half, beating until combined. Stir in the bacon, garlic, blue cheese, and chives. Spoon the mixture evenly into 4 (1-cup) individual baking dishes.

3 Bake in the preheated oven for 15 minutes or until golden and bubbly. Sprinkle evenly with the chopped walnuts. Serve with grapes, flatbread, or assorted crackers.

Prosciutto-Wrapped Asparagus with Citrus Drizzle

(photograph on page 108)

HANDS-ON **20 MINUTES**   TOTAL **40 MINUTES**   SERVES **12**

This is the perfect pickup dish. When putting together a party menu, I always look for something green that guests can easily pop in their mouths without having to get a plate. That's what I call killing two birds with one stone.

12 ounces thinly sliced prosciutto, slices cut in half lengthwise

2 (1-pound) bunches asparagus, trimmed (about 48 asparagus spears)

⅓ cup olive oil

1 tablespoon minced shallot (from 1 shallot)

2 teaspoons Dijon mustard

1 teaspoon lemon zest, plus 3 tablespoons fresh juice (from 1 lemon)

1 teaspoon honey

½ teaspoon kosher salt

½ teaspoon black pepper

1 Preheat the oven to 425°F. Wrap 1 prosciutto half around each asparagus spear. Arrange the wrapped asparagus in a single layer on a lightly greased baking sheet.

2 Bake in the preheated oven until the asparagus is crisp-tender and the prosciutto is browned and crispy, about 20 minutes, rotating the baking sheet halfway through. Arrange the asparagus on a serving platter.

3 Whisk together the oil, shallot, mustard, lemon zest, lemon juice, honey, salt, and pepper; drizzle over the asparagus. Serve immediately.

Mint Chocolate Truffles

HANDS-ON **15 MINUTES**   TOTAL **12 HOURS, 15 MINUTES,**
INCLUDING 12 HOURS CHILLING   SERVES **24**

I wish I kept a running count of how many times I've written "assorted pickup sweets" at the bottom of a catering menu. It's the usual suspects when it comes to cocktail party desserts. You know the ones: lemon squares, chocolate brownies, and chess squares. Mini truffles are just the ticket when you want something bite-size, sweet, and elegant.

⅓ cup plus 2 tablespoons semisweet
   mint chocolate chips
1 (8-ounce) package ⅓-less-fat
   cream cheese, softened

1 (16-ounce) package powdered sugar
¼ cup unsweetened cocoa or sifted
   powdered sugar

1 Place ⅓ cup of the mint chocolate chips in a glass bowl, and microwave at HIGH 1 minute or until almost melted, stirring until smooth. Cool.

2 Add the cream cheese to the melted chocolate chips; beat with an electric mixer at medium speed until smooth. Add 1 package powdered sugar, and beat until well blended. Spread the mixture in an 8-inch square pan; cover and chill 8 hours.

3 Shape the mixture into 1-inch balls, cover, and freeze 3 to 4 hours. Remove from the freezer, and roll the truffles in the cocoa or powdered sugar.

4 Microwave the remaining 2 tablespoons chocolate chips in a small glass bowl, and microwave at HIGH 20 to 30 seconds or until melted.

5 Transfer to a small ziplock plastic bag; seal. Snip a tiny hole in a corner of the bag; drizzle the chocolate over the truffles. Let stand at room temperature 30 minutes before serving.

Note

Freeze the truffles in a single layer in an
airtight container up to 1 month. Let stand at
room temperature 1 hour before serving.

Snowballs

HANDS-ON **45 MINUTES** TOTAL **14 HOURS, 45 MINUTES,
INCLUDING 12 HOURS CHILLING** SERVES **15**

*Snowballs are so fun and festive during the holiday season. These make adorable teachers'
gifts or sweet treats for the mailman or your favorite neighbor. Package them in clear plastic
boxes and tie them with a festive ribbon.*

1 ½ (4-ounce) packages white chocolate
   baking bars, melted according to
   package directions
1 (8-ounce) package cream cheese,
   softened

¾ cup crushed coconut cookies
   (such as Pepperidge Farm)
1 tablespoon coconut rum (or use water)
⅛ teaspoon kosher salt
1 ½ cups shredded coconut

1 Beat the chocolate and cream cheese with a heavy-duty electric stand mixer at
    medium speed until smooth. Add the crushed cookies, coconut rum, and salt,
    beating just until blended. Spread in a parchment paper-lined 9-inch pie plate;
    cover and chill 2 hours.

2 Shape into 1-inch balls (about 2 teaspoons per ball), and place in a single layer in
    a parchment paper-lined jelly-roll pan. Cover and chill 12 to 24 hours.

3 Roll the balls in coconut; chill 1 hour before serving. Refrigerate in a single layer
    in a container up to 1 week.

NIBBLES

&

NOSH

DIRTY
MARTINI

+

ASSORTED
CHEESES

+

PICKLES
AND OLIVES

+

BREAD AND
CRACKERS

NIBBLES & NOSH

If you don't remember anything else from this book, remember this: Friends who come to your home for a party are not there to pass judgment. They are there to enjoy a strong cocktail or a big glass of wine and a nibble. They are your friends and are grateful just to be invited. Too often we get wrapped up trying to create a perfect image of our home and family so we give up altogether and don't extend invitations to the people we adore the most.

When Luke and I first got married, I spent the hours before guests arrived in "party mode" as he called it, running around the house like my hair was on fire. I trapped dust bunnies, fluffed pillows, laid sod, cleaned baseboards, and barked orders at Luke. It was miserable for anyone in my orbit. By the time my friends got there, I was absolutely miserable and exhausted.

It wasn't until we went to one of my friend's homes for a get-together that I had a party epiphany. My friend answered the door with no shoes on and a cat on her shoulder. I walked inside and saw the entire contents of her purse spilled out on the floor. There were dishes in the sink and dust tumbleweeds under the chairs. Yet Kim was so relaxed and at ease. The wine she poured was good and cold and served with the most amazing array of cheeses, charcuterie, and spreads—it seemed effortless. I have never been anywhere that I've had more fun. All of our closest friends were there and just grateful to be together enjoying each other's company. That's when it hit me. Parties aren't about the fuss; they are about friendships. I'm not going to sit here and say that I don't get in "party mode" anymore because I'd be a big fat liar. Having guests over can be stressful. Just try to remember that you are inviting your friends over, and the more relaxed and fun that you are, the more relaxed and fun your party will be!

Dirty Martini

HANDS-ON **5 MINUTES**   TOTAL **5 MINUTES**   SERVES **6**

The dirty part of this recipe refers to the olive juice that can be added to the martini. When I was in college, I thought it was sophisticated to drink martinis. The problem is that I don't like gin or vodka. Honestly, I just liked the glass. My brilliant idea was to ask the bartender to make the martini filthy. Not just dirty, but filthy. I woke up the next day and felt like my mouth had been upholstered with crushed velvet. That quickly ended my martini-drinking days.

1 ½ cups (12 ounces) dry gin or vodka

6 tablespoons (3 ounces) dry vermouth

¼ cup olive brine

Crushed ice

Pitted green olives

Jarred cocktail onions

Lemon peel twists

For each serving, combine ¼ cup of the gin, 1 tablespoon of the vermouth, and 2 teaspoons of the olive brine in a cocktail shaker with ½ cup of crushed ice, and shake until thoroughly chilled, about 30 seconds. Strain into a cocktail glass; serve with the green olives, cocktail onions, or lemon peel twists.

PARTY RULE NO. 5

Have a toast (or two) in your back pocket

"Life is all memory, except for the one present moment that goes by you so quick you hardly catch it going." –Tennessee Williams

Cheese Board

HANDS-ON **10 MINUTES**   TOTAL **10 MINUTES**   SERVES **30**

*Oh no! Guests are coming over and you don't have the time or energy to cook. Here is your
saving grace: One sweep through the gourmet cheese aisle, a few boxes of fancy crackers,
a bag of dried apricots, salted nuts, and fig jam, and suddenly you have one posh party
platter on your hands.*

1 (8-ounce) double-cream Brie round

1 (8-ounce) Parmigiano-Reggiano wedge

1 (8-ounce) Sage Derby wedge

1 (8-ounce) Huntsman cheese (Double
  Gloucester with Blue Stilton) wedge

2 (1-pound) bunches seedless grapes

2 ripe pears, cored and sliced

1 (6-ounce) package dried apricots

1 (13-ounce) jar fig preserves (or use honey)

1 (15-ounce) package salted mixed nuts

4 (12-ounce) boxes assorted party crackers

1 (16-ounce) baguette, thinly sliced

1 cup cornichon pickles

2 cups assorted marinated olives

Arrange cheeses, fruit preserves, nuts, crackers, baguette slices, pickles, and olives on
  a large platter or serving board.

COCKTAILS
& CANAPÉS

OLD FASHIONED

SMOKED SALMON
CANAPÉS

HOT CHEESE
SQUARES

EGG SALAD ON
TOAST POINTS

CUCUMBER ROUNDS WITH
GOAT CHEESE AND
SUN-DRIED TOMATOES

COCKTAILS & CANAPÉS

I love everything about a one- or two-bite canapé. The name sounds so uptown and cosmopolitan, which may seem at odds with the Mississippi Delta. You'd be surprised how many here have traveled the globe, and are extremely well read and worldly. My mama, who grew up overseas, raised me with an appreciation for all things European. I can remember her pronouncing words like crudité and canapé in a thick French accent. Of course, she would end the sentence with "y'all." Mama was a beautiful hostess. She passed around silver trays with tiny little bites so beautifully prepared and garnished so perfectly that they looked like little presents, each one a tiny surprise.

At my catering company, we wouldn't dare start a party without passing around two canapés. The little appetizers are a lovely icebreaker to get a party in gear. They are extremely economical too. (A nice way of saying what I'm really thinking—that they are cheap, cheap, cheap.) After all, a canapé is tiny—you can use very little of the expensive goods. Think: a little lump crabmeat on a cucumber round, smoked salmon on a deviled egg, shrimp on a bamboo pick, or caviar on an endive leaf. The options are endless. I mean, my word, Martha Stewart wrote an entire book on the subject.

If you're planning a party that revolves around cocktails and canapés, you need to make damn sure the cocktails are tasty and plentiful and that you don't skimp on the canapés. You would never want your guests to leave thinking you were chintzy.

Beer, wine, and maybe a specialty cocktail or two will suffice. Just make sure you have at least six different canapés. Two for vegetarian friends, two for the meat eaters, and two that include seafood. Pass trays for the first 30 minutes of the party and then place the trays around the room so guests can help themselves. Some people are a little apprehensive about taking a canapé off a tray but will belly up once it's on a coffee table or sideboard. Now go plan this fun party and start practicing your French accent!

Old Fashioned

HANDS-ON **5 MINUTES**   TOTAL **5 MINUTES**   SERVES **8**

There are so many newfangled bitters on the market, and it's so fun to let your guests experiment with them. This Old Fashioned is the perfect cocktail to jazz up with a splash of bacon bitters. Southern Comfort is a whiskey-based liqueur that adds a fruit-meets-spice twist that is a nice alternative to the traditional recipe made with bourbon or rye whiskey.

½ cup water

8 drops of Angostura bitters

4 teaspoons granulated sugar (optional)

1 ½ cups (12 ounces) bourbon or
    Southern Comfort

Orange slices

Maraschino cherries with stems

For each serving, stir together 1 tablespoon of water, 1 drop of the bitters, and, if desired, ½ teaspoon of the sugar in an old-fashioned glass. Add 2 ice cubes. Add 3 tablespoons of the bourbon, and stir. Serve with an orange slice and a cherry.

124

Smoked Salmon Canapés

HANDS-ON **10 MINUTES**   TOTAL **20 MINUTES**   SERVES **12**

These light bites are in a class of their own. Make sure that the baguette is thin enough that even after it's sliced, toasted, and topped with salmon, it's still only one bite. There is nothing worse than a canapé that takes two bites to finish. It's almost inevitable that you will take one bite and the other half of the canapé will make its way down the front of your dress.

1 (16-ounce) baguette

8 ounces thinly sliced smoked salmon

1 (8-ounce) package cream cheese, softened

½ cup sour cream

24 dill sprigs

1 Preheat the oven to 400°F. Cut the baguette into 24 (½-inch-thick) slices, and place on a baking sheet.

2 Bake in the preheated oven for 5 minutes or until lightly toasted; remove to wire racks to cool.

3 Cut the salmon into 24 pieces. Spread the baguette slices evenly with the cream cheese, and top evenly with the smoked salmon and sour cream. Place a dill sprig on each canapé.

Hot Cheese Squares

HANDS-ON **15 MINUTES**   TOTAL **8 HOURS, 45 MINUTES,**
INCLUDING 8 HOURS CHILLING   SERVES **18**

I almost died when I saw this recipe. This is my Great-Aunt Joy's recipe, and when she served it at a fancy gathering I begged for the recipe, and she gave it to me! Her daughter was furious because she refused to give it to her! I have held onto that handwritten recipe through countless moves, and I've guarded it with my life. I honestly thought we were the only two people in the world who knew how to make this recipe. Then I opened page 365 of the original Southern Living Party Cookbook, *and thought well, well, well, Aunt Joy you have some explaining to do!*

1 (16-ounce) white bread loaf, unsliced

½ cup (4 ounces) salted butter, melted

3 ounces cream cheese, softened

1 ounce sharp Cheddar cheese, shredded (about ¼ cup)

2 large egg whites

Thyme sprigs

1 Trim the crusts from the bread. Cut into 3 (1-inch-thick) slices, stack the slices, and then cut the slices into 6 squares.

2 Melt the butter, cream cheese, and Cheddar cheese in a saucepan over medium heat, whisking often until smooth. Let cool 15 minutes.

3 Beat the egg whites with an electric mixer at high speed until stiff; fold into the cooled cheese mixture. Spread the cheese mixture on all sides of the bread squares; place on baking sheets lined with parchment paper. Cover and chill overnight. (Squares may be frozen at this point, and thawed and cooked later.)

4 Preheat the oven to 400°F. Uncover the cheese squares, and bake in the preheated oven until browned, about 15 minutes; serve hot, garnished with thyme sprigs, if desired.

Egg Salad on Toast Points

(photograph on page 126)

HANDS-ON **25 MINUTES**   TOTAL **25 MINUTES**   SERVES **12**

Egg salad is often overlooked, and I'm on a mission to bring it back. The deviled egg has become the darling of the party circuit, but its cousin egg salad is really where it's at. It's just as versatile, a bit more elegant, and the perfect complement for a toast point.

²/₃ cup mayonnaise

4 large hard-cooked eggs, peeled
    and chopped

1 celery stalk, diced

4 bacon slices, cooked and crumbled

¼ cup chopped fresh chives

1 tablespoon minced sweet onion

¼ teaspoon seasoned salt

½ teaspoon freshly ground black pepper

12 very thin white or wheat sandwich
    bread slices, lightly toasted

1 cup firmly packed fresh spinach (optional)

Whole fresh chives

1 Stir together ⅓ cup of the mayonnaise, eggs, celery, bacon, chopped chives, onion, salt, and pepper. Spread the remaining ⅓ cup mayonnaise evenly over 1 side of each bread slice.

2 Layer spinach evenly on top of bread slices, if desired. Spread bread slices, mayonnaise side up, evenly with egg salad. Cut bread slices in half diagonally. Garnish with whole chives, if desired.

SWEET-PICKLE EGG SALAD CLUB: Omit the bacon and chives. Add 2 tablespoons instant potato flakes and 1 tablespoon sweet pickle relish. Proceed with the recipe as directed.

SHRIMP-EGG SALAD CLUB: Omit the bacon. Add ⅔ cup finely chopped boiled shrimp, ½ teaspoon lemon zest, and ¼ teaspoon cayenne pepper. Proceed with the recipe as directed.

Cucumber Rounds with Goat Cheese and Sun-Dried Tomatoes

(photograph on page 126)

HANDS-ON **15 MINUTES**   TOTAL **15 MINUTES**   SERVES **8**

My first job was at a Putt Putt Golf and Games. My second job was working for Another Roadside Attraction Catering Company. I was in high school, and we got paid in cash. I was in heaven. This recipe was their go-to passed hors d'oeuvre. When I started my own company this quickly became my go-to as well.

2 English cucumbers

2 (4-ounce) logs goat cheese, softened

4 ounces cream cheese, softened

2 tablespoons minced fresh chives, plus more for garnish

1 teaspoon lemon zest, plus 1 tablespoon fresh juice (from 1 lemon)

1 garlic clove, minced (about 1 teaspoon)

½ teaspoon kosher salt

¼ teaspoon black pepper

½ cup sun-dried tomatoes with herbs in oil, thinly sliced

1 Peel the cucumbers, leaving a few green stripes of peel; cut into ½-inch-thick diagonal slices.

2 Place the goat cheese, cream cheese, 2 tablespoons minced chives, lemon zest, lemon juice, garlic, salt, and pepper in a medium bowl. Beat with an electric mixer at medium speed until well combined and fluffy, about 3 to 5 minutes. Spoon the goat cheese mixture into a pastry bag, and pipe evenly onto the cucumber slices. Top with the sun-dried tomato slivers. Garnish with chives, if desired.

Canapé Carnival...
Mini More Options!

No one wants to juggle a fork, plate, napkin, glass, and a witty conversation. One-or two-bite appetizers are the jewels that make a great cocktail party sparkle. A thoughtful roundup of delicious bites will surprise and delight while satisfying guests. Think beyond the skewered meatball or standard pig-in-blanket with even more of our favorite finger foods.

Chicken Salad Tarts

Crisp **1 (1.9-ounce) package frozen mini phyllo pastry shells** according to package directions; cool. Spoon **¾ cup store-bought chicken salad** into cooled shells. Gently place **1 fresh mango sliver** onto chicken salad in each shell, shaping mango sliver to resemble a flower. Place **1 small piece of blackberry** and **1 small basil sprig** next to each mango slice. **Makes 15 tarts**

Crab Cake Hush Puppies

Stir together **1 cup self-rising white cornmeal mix, ½ cup self-rising flour, 3 thinly sliced scallions, ¼ cup finely chopped red bell pepper, 1 tablespoon sugar,** and **¼ teaspoon salt** in a large bowl. Stir in **8 ounces fresh lump crabmeat,** picked free of shell; **1 large egg;** and **¾ cup beer** until just moistened. Let stand 10 minutes. Pour **oil to depth of 2 inches** into a Dutch oven; heat to 360°F. Drop batter by tablespoonfuls into hot oil, and fry, in batches, 2 to 3 minutes or until golden brown, turning once. Serve with your favorite rémoulade or cocktail sauce. **Makes about 32**

Strawberry Pretzel Crostini

Stir together **2 cups finely chopped strawberries, ¼ cup chopped fresh basil, 2 tablespoons dark brown sugar, 4 teaspoons minced shallot,** and a **pinch of black pepper.** Spread **1 (3-ounce) package softened cream cheese** onto **36 pretzel crackers.** Top with the strawberry mixture. **Makes 3 dozen**

Andouille Mini Dogs

Sauté **1 (12-ounce) package Cajun-style andouille miniature sausages or cocktail-size smoked sausages** in **1 tablespoon hot olive oil over** medium 5 minutes or until lightly browned and thoroughly heated. Cut slits in tops of **1 (9.25-ounce) package dinner rolls,** warmed. Fill each roll with 1 sausage, and top with **Creole mustard** and **sweet pepper relish. Makes about 25**

Mint Julep Jigglers

Sprinkle **2 envelopes unflavored gelatin** over **2 cups cold water** in a medium saucepan. Let stand 5 minutes. Add **½ cup firmly packed fresh mint leaves** and **½ cup granulated sugar.** Cook over medium-high, stirring often, 3 to 5 minutes or until steaming. Let stand 15 minutes. Remove and discard mint leaves. Stir in **1 cup bourbon.** Pour the mixture into a lightly greased 9- x 5-inch loaf pan. Chill 4 hours to 1 week. Cut into squares. Garnish with **fresh mint sprigs** and **coarse sparkling sugar. Makes 18**

133

Boiled Peanut Hummus

Process **1 cup shelled spicy boiled peanuts, ¼ cup water, 2 tablespoons chopped fresh cilantro, 2 tablespoons fresh lime juice, 2 tablespoons olive oil, 2 tablespoons creamy peanut butter, 1 ½ teaspoons hot sauce, 1 teaspoon minced fresh garlic,** and **¼ teaspoon ground cumin** in a food processor 1 minute or until smooth. Spoon into shot glasses or small bowls, and drizzle with **olive oil.** Sprinkle with **black pepper.** Serve with **carrot** or **celery sticks.** Garnish with **fresh cilantro sprigs. Makes 1 ½ cups**

AFTER-THEATER NIGHTCAP

It's been said that if the party is over and you look around and the Heiskells are still there, you have outstayed your welcome. This was especially true when we lived in the Delta. We had known most of our friends for years, and they might as well have been family. The only other couple in town that also didn't know when to go home was the Dossets. If our eyes met and we realized that the four of us were the last ones there, we would make a mad dash to the door so we wouldn't (once again) be the last man standing at the party.

In Oxford, my hometown, the bars close at 12 a.m. Lord knows the college kids don't even go out until 9 or 10 p.m. That's not much time out, which is fine by me. My daddy has always said that nothing good happens after midnight. His other quote was, "Darling, leave while you are still having fun."

When the Oxford bars close, college kids walk to the Chevron to buy as many pizza rolls, chicken-on-a-sticks, egg rolls, and deep-fried burritos as their little hands can hold while juggling a couple cases of beer. They revel in fried food and Natural Light at some off-campus house until the sun comes up.

This after-theater nightcap is a much more refined late night for adults who still have a college kid trapped deep inside or, who like the Heiskells and Dossets, just don't know when to call it a night!

This party is so easy to pull together. Before you go to the theater or concert, put out all of the food that is safe at room temperature. If you plan to serve something cold, go ahead and put it on a platter and make space for it in the fridge. Have the bar completely set up, except for the ice bucket. The coolers should be filled with wine or Champagne and beer on ice, so it's cold and ready when guests arrive. Don't lollygag after the show. Make a beeline to your house, light candles, fill the ice bucket, set out the cold platters, take a deep breath, and let the fun begin.

Brandy Alexanders

HANDS-ON **5 MINUTES**   TOTAL **5 MINUTES**   SERVES **8**

Memphis, Tennessee, is famous for barbecue, blues, and the Mississippi River. But for me, it will always be famous for the elegant Justine's restaurant. Justine's was the fanciest place I had ever been. It was like going into a jewelry box for dinner. The menu was classic French, and we ended every meal with their famous dessert that was layered with brandy and ice cream. This set into motion the obsession with after-dinner drinks, like this Brandy Alexander, at the young age of ten.

1 ½ cups (12 ounces) brandy

¾ cup (6 ounces) crème de cacao

½ cup half-and-half

Crushed ice

Freshly grated nutmeg (optional)

For each serving, combine 3 tablespoons of the brandy, 1 ½ tablespoons of the crème de cacao, and 1 tablespoon of the half-and-half in a cocktail shaker; add ½ cup crushed ice, cover with the lid, and shake until thoroughly chilled, about 30 seconds. Strain into a cocktail glass. Garnish with nutmeg, if desired.

1972 SOUTHERN LIVING PARTY COOKBOOK ORIGINAL

AFTER-THEATER
★ NIGHT ★

Brandy Alexander

Coffee Service
with Irish Whiskey

Salted

Coffee Service with Irish Whiskey

We catered a wedding for an adorable bride from Memphis. She was marrying a lovely groom from Ireland. At the reception, we served only wine, beer, and Irish whiskey. At every planning meeting we had with the happy couple, they kept telling me that I needed to triple the amount of whiskey we would normally serve. I really didn't listen. I'm from the Mississippi Delta, and we know about heavy drinking. We did double the amount but then ran out after 45 minutes, and then we went to the liquor store four times more for Irish whiskey. If you invite an Irish man over for this party, heed my warning and stock up on the whiskey.

Heavy cream and whipped cream

Peppermint sticks

Chocolate shavings

Cocoa powder

Ground cinnamon

Ground nutmeg

Ground cardamom

Pumpkin pie spice

White and brown sugar cubes

Flavored syrups

**Airplane-size bottles of liquors
and liqueurs, such as bourbon,
Irish whiskey, Kahlúa, amaretto,
brandy, Frangelico**

Lemon zest strips

Note

A hot coffee station is a terrific way to let your guests
get creative while serving themselves. Place bowls
of add-ins and shakers of spices next to the coffee urn.
We have been known to fill silver punch bowls with
airplane-size bottles of assorted liquors for guests
who wish to spike their brew. Hair of the dog!

Almond-Butter Cookies

(photograph on page 138)

HANDS-ON **40 MINUTES**   TOTAL **1 HOUR, 40 MINUTES**   SERVES **54**

What I love most about these cookies is that they freeze beautifully. Even better, this recipe makes a ton, so you can have them on hand when unexpected guests come over. Let the cookies cool after baking, arrange them in a plastic container, and place them in the freezer. When you are ready to serve, remove the cookies from the freezer, let them thaw, and then dust with powdered sugar.

1 cup (8 ounces) unsalted butter, softened

²/₃ cup granulated sugar

½ teaspoon vanilla extract

¼ teaspoon almond extract

2 ¼ cups (about 9 ⅝ ounces) all-purpose flour

1 cup coarsely ground blanched almonds

¼ teaspoon table salt

Blanched whole almonds, toasted

1 Preheat the oven to 350°F. Beat together the butter and granulated sugar with an electric mixer at medium speed until combined; add the vanilla and almond extracts. Beat in the flour, ground almonds, and salt until combined.

2 Form the dough into balls about the size of a quarter, and place 2 inches apart on a baking sheet lined with parchment paper. Press each dough ball with the bottom of a glass to flatten; press 1 almond firmly in the top of each cookie.

3 Bake in the preheated oven until golden, about 10 minutes. Let cool for 1 minute. Transfer the cookies to a plate.

Butterscotch Bars

(photograph on page 138)

HANDS-ON **15 MINUTES**   TOTAL **1 HOUR**   SERVES **36**

We frequently turn to this bar whenever we are looking for new and exciting pickup sweets to put on a cocktail menu. There are so many chocolate and lemon desserts that repeatedly appear on buffets, so it's nice to have a change of pace, and this butterscotch bar really fits the bill.

CRUST

¾ cup packed light brown sugar

½ cup (4 ounces) unsalted butter, softened

1 ½ cups (6 ⅜ ounces) all-purpose flour

¼ teaspoon table salt

TOPPING

1 cup butterscotch chips

¼ cup dark corn syrup

2 tablespoons (1 ounce) unsalted butter

1 tablespoon water

½ teaspoon table salt

2 cups coarsely chopped walnuts

1   Prepare the Crust: Preheat the oven to 375°F. Beat together the sugar and butter with an electric mixer at medium speed until well blended. Add the flour and salt, and beat until a dough is formed. Press into an ungreased 13- x 9-inch baking pan. Bake in the preheated oven for 10 minutes.

2   Prepare the Topping: Combine the butterscotch chips, corn syrup, butter, 1 tablespoon water, and salt in a microwave-safe bowl. Microwave on HIGH 45 seconds, and then stir well. If needed, microwave for another 30 seconds; stir until smooth. Stir in the chopped walnuts until combined.

3   Spread the Topping evenly over the Crust, and bake in the preheated oven until bubbly, about 10 minutes. Let cool 5 minutes. Score the bars while warm. Let cool 20 minutes, and then cut into bars. Freeze, if desired.

Salted Butter Pecan Bites

HANDS-ON **25 MINUTES**   TOTAL **1 HOUR, 5 MINUTES**   SERVES **24**

When my friend Jincy and I started our first business, we called it "Instead of Flowers." For example, if someone died or had a baby, our clients would call us instead of ordering flowers, and we would deliver food. We had so much fun with this company that our husbands used to call our business "Instead of a Job!" Jincy's job was to make these pecan bites because, for the life of me, I ruined them every time. They aren't difficult, but you have to watch the butter, sugar, and cream closely. It takes a little bit of focus, which has never been my strong suit.

1 cup chopped pecans

12 graham crackers

1 cup packed brown sugar

³/₄ cup (6 ounces) salted butter

2 tablespoons whipping cream

1 teaspoon vanilla extract

¹/₄ teaspoon kosher salt

1 Preheat the oven to 350°F. Bake the pecans in a single layer in a shallow pan 10 to 12 minutes or until toasted and fragrant, stirring halfway through.

2 Line a 15- x 10-inch jelly-roll pan with aluminum foil; lightly grease the foil. Arrange the graham crackers in a single layer in the prepared pan, slightly overlapping the edges.

3 Combine the sugar, butter, and cream in a medium-size heavy saucepan; bring to a boil over medium, stirring occasionally. Remove from the heat, and stir in the vanilla and pecans. Pour the butter mixture over the crackers, spreading to coat.

4 Bake in the preheated oven for 10 to 11 minutes or until lightly browned and bubbly. Immediately sprinkle with the salt, and slide the foil from the pan onto a wire rack. Cool completely, about 30 minutes. Break into bite-size pieces.

cheers MY dears

Prosecco-
Elderflower Cocktail

Pickled Shrimp

Salmon Mousse

Stuffed Endive Leaves
with Goat Cheese

Cheese Straw
Tomato Tartlets

Caramel Meringue Cookies

Seven-Layer Cookies

CHEERS MY DEARS

MENU FOR 12

There is so much truth in the phrase "It takes a village to raise a child." I was blessed with amazing friends whose mothers were just as amazing. I didn't realize just how great their mothers were until I had my own children. I shudder every time I think about the sleepless nights our moms endured as they waited for us to come home.

I've hardly been able to look Melinda Yarbrough in the eye since the night our friend Sharon wanted to break up with her boyfriend. She finally got the nerve up at 1 a.m., which was well past our curfew. We knew he was at a party, so we had no other option but to sneak out of the house to find him. We rolled Mendy's car down the driveway in neutral with the lights off. We got to the party and Sharon began the breakup talk with her boyfriend. Mendy, Jill, and I decided to take full advantage of being out and enjoyed ourselves.

Meanwhile, Mendy's mom, Melinda, woke up and realized that we were gone. There were no cellphones then so she stayed up and waited and waited and waited. She was so sick with worry that she devoured two bags of Hershey's Kisses. Back we came, up the driveway with the lights off, and were shocked to see Melinda standing in the kitchen. We'd put that woman through hell. Now that I have children and I realize how our poor mothers suffered, it's only right that we have a party to celebrate them (or what's left of them) after raising us.

The guest list for this party should include your very best friends from childhood and their mothers. Sure this is about the food and the bubbly, but its main purpose is to share stories and then apologize over and over again. It's about letting the lovely ladies know what an impact their kindness had on our lives. This menu is simple. It's stuff you put out and forget about. The focus is on storytelling not replenishing hors d'oeuvres. Find an old photo of you and your best buddies from high school and frame it in a pretty silver frame engraved with "Our deepest apologies and love." It's a fun gift for the moms who raised us so well!

Prosecco-Elderflower Cocktail

(photograph on page 149)

HANDS-ON **5 MINUTES**   TOTAL **5 MINUTES**   SERVES **12**

St-Germain makes a lovely elderflower liqueur. The elderflower blossoms that grow on the hillsides in France are gathered. Once the flowers have been collected, the blossoms are macerated to extract all the flavor. This process is a guarded family secret. I am not too terribly concerned about uncovering this secret; I am only concerned when I get to the end of the bottle.

12 fresh strawberries, hulled and
   thinly sliced
12 large, ripe fresh strawberries,
   stems removed
12 mint leaves

1 ½ cups (12 ounces) elderflower
   liqueur (such as St-Germain)
¾ cup fresh lemon juice (from
   3 lemons)
6 cups ice
2 (750-milliliter) bottles Prosecco

1 Divide the strawberry slices evenly among 12 (8- to 10-ounce) wineglasses, and set aside the glasses while you make the cocktail.

2 For every 2 servings, muddle 2 of the whole strawberries with 2 of the mint leaves in the bottom of a cocktail shaker. Add ¼ cup of the elderflower liqueur, 2 tablespoons of the lemon juice, and 1 cup ice. Cover with the lid, and shake vigorously until thoroughly chilled, about 30 seconds; strain into glasses. Top each serving with ⅓ cup Prosecco, and serve immediately.

Note

Other liqueurs with a floral note that
would make a great substitute for the
elderflower liqueur used here include:

Koval Jasmine Liqueur
Fruitlab Hibiscus Liqueur
Crispin's Rose Liqueur

Pickled Shrimp

(photograph on page 149)

HANDS-ON **35 MINUTES**   TOTAL **45 MINUTES**   SERVES **20**

I prefer to use fresh shrimp for this recipe, but you can also use frozen if you'd like. When purchasing frozen shrimp, please make note of the label. You want to ensure the package comes from the United States, and that the only ingredient listed is shrimp. Some companies add a solution to extend the life of the frozen shrimp. Not a bad idea in theory, but the problem is that it completely ruins the consistency of the shrimp. Okay, I will climb down off my soapbox now.

3 pounds large unpeeled, raw shrimp

½ cup chopped celery leaves

¼ cup pickling spice

3 ½ teaspoons table salt

2 cups thinly sliced Vidalia onion
   (from 1 large onion)

8 bay leaves

¼ cup olive oil

3 tablespoons fresh lemon juice
   (from 1 lemon)

1 Place the shrimp in a large pot; cover with boiling water. Add the celery leaves, pickling spice, and 3 teaspoons of the salt; cover and bring to a simmer over high. Cook until the shrimp are pink, about 2 minutes, adding the onions during the last 30 seconds of cooking time to soften slightly. Drain the shrimp and onions, and place in a bowl of ice water. Let stand 30 seconds. Peel the shrimp, leaving the tails on.

2 Arrange the shrimp, onion slices, and bay leaves in a shallow dish. Whisk together the olive oil, lemon juice, and remaining ½ teaspoon salt in a small bowl; drizzle over the shrimp to marinate. Chill up to 4 hours.

Salmon Mousse

HANDS-ON **15 MINUTES**   TOTAL **3 HOURS, 15 MINUTES**   SERVES **12**

If you are lucky enough to have gelatin molds passed down to you, keep them. These molds look like tube or Bundt pans used to bake pound cakes. They are often made of copper and have an embossed pattern on the bottom. Every time I flip one of these mold pans over I do a little booty-shaking dance, say a prayer, and then I carefully remove the pan. It's my good luck ritual. I haven't lost a gelatin mold yet.

½ cup heavy cream

⅔ cup water

1 (¼-ounce) envelope unflavored gelatin

½ cup finely chopped celery (from 1 stalk)

¼ cup finely chopped red bell pepper (from 1 bell pepper)

¼ cup finely chopped yellow bell pepper (from 1 bell pepper)

¼ cup mayonnaise

¼ cup sour cream

3 tablespoons finely chopped scallions

1 tablespoon chopped fresh tarragon

2 teaspoons lemon zest, plus 1 tablespoon fresh juice (from 1 lemon)

½ teaspoon kosher salt

8 ounces skinless smoked salmon, finely chopped (about 2 cups)

Toast points, toasted baguette slices, assorted crackers or crudités for serving

1 Beat the cream in a medium bowl with an electric mixer at high speed until soft peaks form; cover and chill.

2 Place ⅔ cup water in a small saucepan. Sprinkle the gelatin over the water, and let stand until softened, about 5 minutes. Cook over low, stirring constantly, just until the gelatin is dissolved, about 5 minutes. Remove from the heat, and cool 5 minutes.

3 Add the celery, bell peppers, mayonnaise, sour cream, scallions, tarragon, lemon zest, lemon juice, and salt, stirring well to combine. Fold in the salmon and whipped cream, continuing to fold until all the ingredients are well incorporated.

4 Pour the mixture into a plastic wrap-lined 9- x 5-inch loaf pan. Cover and chill at least 3 hours before unmolding. Serve with the toast points, toasted baguette slices, crackers, or crudités.

Stuffed Endive Leaves with Goat Cheese

HANDS-ON **15 MINUTES**   TOTAL **15 MINUTES**   SERVES **12**

These little leaves make the perfect boat for any pass-around hors d'oeuvre. They are also lovely topped with smoked salmon and a little piece of sun-dried tomato and basil for garnish.

1 ounce goat cheese, crumbled
  (about ¼ cup)

2 ounces cream cheese, softened
  (about ¼ cup)

1 teaspoon lemon zest, plus 1 tablespoon
  fresh juice (from 1 lemon)

¼ teaspoon kosher salt

¼ teaspoon black pepper

2 ½ tablespoons thinly sliced fresh chives

1 ½ tablespoons finely chopped
  fresh flat-leaf parsley

2 ½ teaspoons finely chopped
  fresh tarragon

24 red and green Belgian endive leaves
  (about 2 heads)

1 Stir together the goat cheese, cream cheese, lemon zest, lemon juice, salt, pepper, 2 tablespoons of the chives, 1 tablespoon of the parsley, and 2 teaspoons of the tarragon in a bowl.

2 Arrange the endive leaves on a platter. Spoon heaping teaspoonfuls of the mixture into the bottom halves of each endive leaf.

3 Combine the remaining ½ tablespoon each chives and parsley and ½ teaspoon tarragon and sprinkle evenly over the stuffed leaves. Serve immediately.

Cheese Straw Tomato Tartlets

HANDS-ON **30 MINUTES**   TOTAL **3 HOURS, 25 MINUTES**   SERVES **24**

This recipe combines my two favorite foods to make one amazing, savory pickup bite. Feel free to adjust the amount of crushed red pepper added to the dough to suit your fancy.

CRUST

2 ½ cups (about 10 ⅝ ounces)
 all-purpose flour

½ teaspoon kosher salt

¼ to ½ teaspoon crushed red pepper

¾ cup (6 ounces) cold salted butter,
 cut into pieces

6 ounces extra-sharp white Cheddar
 cheese, shredded (about 1 ½ cups)

½ to ¾ cup ice-cold water

FILLING

2 pints red and yellow cherry or grape
 tomatoes, cut in half lengthwise

3 garlic cloves, finely chopped

2 tablespoons chopped fresh basil

1 tablespoon chopped fresh oregano

1 tablespoon chopped fresh flat-leaf parsley

2 tablespoons red wine vinegar

2 tablespoons extra-virgin olive oil

1 teaspoon kosher salt

¼ teaspoon freshly ground black pepper

Crumbled feta or shaved Parmesan cheese

1 Prepare the Crust: Pulse the flour, salt, and crushed red pepper in a food processor 3 or 4 times or until combined. Add the butter, and pulse 5 or 6 times or until crumbly. Stir in the cheese. With the processor running, gradually add ½ cup ice-cold water, and process until the dough forms a ball and pulls away from the sides of the bowl, adding more water, 1 tablespoon at a time, if necessary.

2 Divide the dough in half; place each half on a large piece of plastic wrap. Shape each into a flat disk. Wrap in the plastic wrap, and chill 2 to 24 hours.

3 Prepare the Filling: Toss together the tomatoes, garlic, basil, oregano, parsley, vinegar, oil, salt, and pepper in a medium bowl; let stand 1 to 1 ½ hours.

4 Preheat the oven to 400°F. Roll 1 dough disk to ¼-inch thickness on a lightly floured surface. Cut into 12 rounds using a 2 ½-inch round cutter, rerolling the dough as needed; press into the cups of a lightly greased 12-cup miniature muffin pan. (The dough will come slightly up the sides.) Repeat the procedure with the remaining dough disk and another muffin pan. Divide the tomato mixture among the cups.

5 Bake in the preheated oven for 40 to 45 minutes or until golden. Remove from the pans. Cool completely on a wire rack, about 15 minutes. Sprinkle with the cheese.

Caramel Meringue Cookies

HANDS-ON **30 MINUTES** TOTAL **1 HOUR, 10 MINUTES** SERVES **12**

These caramel cookies are as light as a feather. If you are not careful, you could devour a whole batch without even realizing it. If they become too tempting, they do freeze well.

1 large egg white

⅛ teaspoon cream of tartar

¾ cup packed light brown sugar

1 tablespoon all-purpose flour

¾ cup chopped pecans or walnuts

½ teaspoon vanilla extract

1 Preheat the oven to 325°F. Beat the egg white with an electric mixer at medium speed until foamy. Add the cream of tartar, and beat at medium speed until soft peaks form. Beat in the sugar, 1 tablespoon at a time, until stiff peaks form. Fold in the flour until fully incorporated. Fold in the nuts and vanilla. Let the mixture stand 5 minutes.

2 Drop the mixture by teaspoonfuls, 2 inches apart, onto a greased baking sheet. Bake in the preheated oven until firm, about 10 minutes. Cool on the baking sheet 5 minutes; transfer to a wire rack to cool completely, about 20 minutes. Store in an airtight container up to 1 week.

Note

When baking the meringues, don't open the oven
after turning it off; this will help them dry
to airy perfection without residual stickiness.
And don't attempt them on a humid or rainy day.

Seven-Layer Cookies

HANDS-ON **20 MINUTES**   TOTAL **55 MINUTES**   SERVES **24**

Okay, so there is no excuse in this whole world that could explain why someone would not make this cookie. In all of my years of cooking and entertaining, I cannot say that I have found an easier recipe. For goodness sake, you don't even have to stir anything. Layer, bake, done!

⅓ cup (3 ounces) salted butter

1 ½ cups graham cracker crumbs

1 cup sweetened flaked coconut

1 cup semisweet chocolate chips

1 cup butterscotch chips

1 cup chopped pecans or walnuts

1 (14-ounce) can sweetened
    condensed milk

1 Preheat the oven to 325°F. Place the butter in a 9-inch square pan, and place in the oven while it preheats. Bake until the butter is melted, about 5 minutes.

2 Remove the pan from the oven, and spread the graham cracker crumbs evenly over the butter. Sprinkle the coconut over the graham cracker crumbs followed by the chocolate chips, butterscotch chips, and nuts. (Do not mix the layers.)

3 Pour the condensed milk evenly over the top of the nuts, and bake in the preheated oven until melted through, about 30 minutes (25 minutes if using a glass dish). Let cool. Cut into rectangles.

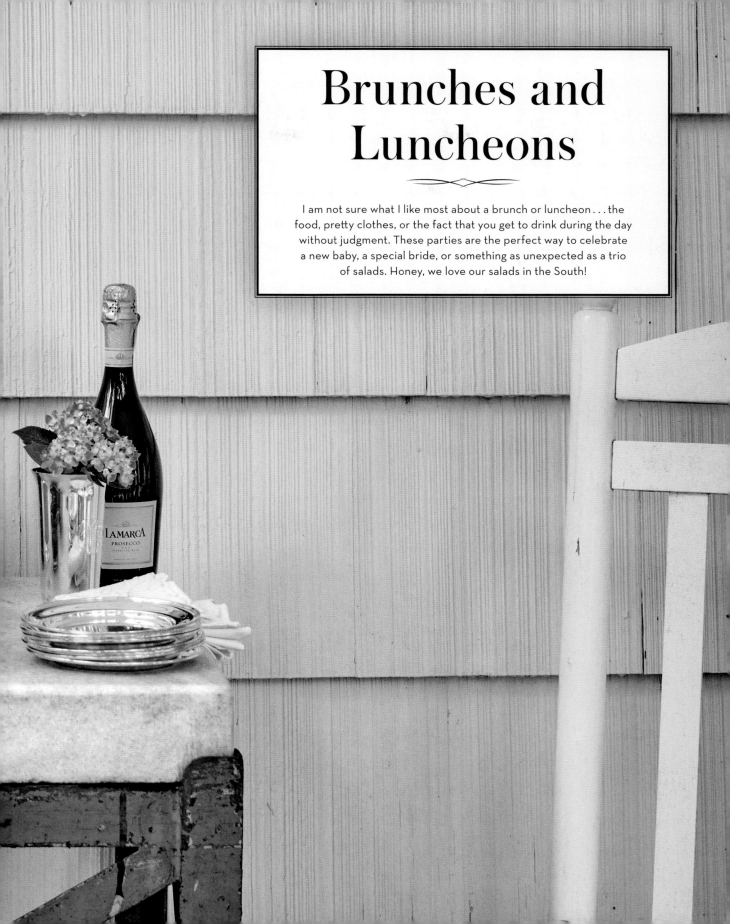

Brunches and Luncheons

I am not sure what I like most about a brunch or luncheon . . . the food, pretty clothes, or the fact that you get to drink during the day without judgment. These parties are the perfect way to celebrate a new baby, a special bride, or something as unexpected as a trio of salads. Honey, we love our salads in the South!

Gospel
Brunch

Fried Pork Chops
Squash and Swiss Cheese Casserole
Hoppin' John
Banana Pudding Pie

GOSPEL BRUNCH

This is beyond a shadow of a doubt my favorite party that I have ever thrown. We weren't really celebrating anything; it was just an ordinary Sunday that was no more special than another. I'd always been intrigued by the idea of having guests come over after church and greeting them with a wonderfully talented, soulful choir that could sing like angels.

My vision was for the members of the choir to line the walkway that leads to the front door of our house, singing their hearts out as guests arrived. As guests walked up they were serenaded like kings and queens. We all gathered on the porch, listened in awe, or sang along as we passed around iced tea, Bloody Marys, and old-fashioned milk punch. When the spirituals and church hymns came to an end, it was time for fellowship around the table. The food setup was reminiscent of the potluck suppers I'd had at the Baptist church in Rosedale. I used my vintage china and pressed linen napkins. The menu was just as soulful and Southern as the gospel choir.

While I adore fried chicken, sometimes it's fun to go with the unexpected like these fried pork chops. These recipes are some of my most favorite Southern staples —a comforting casserole, black-eyed peas, and banana pudding in a pie shell. Feel free to play with this menu to suit your tastes. Even though I planned every detail of the party, I decided to keep the choir a secret. I invited people very casually—calling friends and family a few days before to ask them to come over for a relaxed lunch after church. (It's so fun to keep a few surprises up your sleeve.) The little moments that no one sees coming are much more memorable, and folks, that is the bottom line—making memories and connecting with one another. This party ticks all the boxes.

Fried Pork Chops

HANDS-ON **30 MINUTES**   TOTAL **30 MINUTES**   SERVES **8**

This recipe is extremely basic, but the cooking techniques used here—breading, frying, and making gravy—are the basis for so many wonderful recipes. Master this recipe and you're well on your way to becoming a fine cook.

⅔ cup plus 2 tablespoons
  all-purpose flour
1 teaspoon kosher salt
1 teaspoon black pepper
8 (6-ounce) bone-in pork chops
  (about ½ inch thick)

2 tablespoons olive oil
¼ cup (2 ounces) unsalted butter
½ cup dry white wine
2 cups chicken stock
Fresh flat-leaf parsley leaves
Fresh thyme sprigs (optional)

1 Stir together ⅔ cup of the flour and 1 teaspoon each salt and pepper in a shallow dish. Dredge the pork chops in the flour mixture, evenly coating all sides, shaking off excess.

2 Heat the olive oil in a large skillet over medium-high. Add the pork chops, and cook until golden, about 4 minutes per side. Transfer the pork chops to a platter, and keep warm.

3 Melt the butter in the skillet. Add the remaining 2 tablespoons flour, whisking until smooth. Add the wine, and cook, stirring and scraping to loosen the browned bits from the bottom of the skillet, until the mixture is reduced by about one-third, about 2 minutes. Add the chicken stock; bring to a boil, and reduce the heat to medium-low. Cook, stirring occasionally, until the sauce is thickened, about 4 minutes.

4 Spoon the gravy over the warm pork chops on the platter. Sprinkle the pork chops with the parsley leaves and thyme sprigs, if desired, just before serving.

Brunches

A brunch starts the day in a relaxed festive way. It's a time to appreciate an especially good morning, whether it's just the family on a lazy Saturday or a crowd before the ball game.

The time is as flexible as the feeling, and the hostess is left to choose which hour best suits her, her guests, and the activities that follow. As the noon hour approaches, the dishes move from the egg and bacon sphere to luncheon fare. But for those who can't fathom a brunch without eggs, there are several variations on the ever-popular fluffy scrambled ones.

A brunch suggests a hearty meal, as it is intended to take the place of breakfast and lunch. The heartiness depends on the function. Before a hunt you may see several meats, a variety of eggs and breads, grits and stewed tomatoes. But after a morning wedding, a brunch would most likely resemble a light but elegant luncheon.

For a start, those who really haven't had breakfast appreciate something refreshing, a juice or fruit perhaps. And to add a bit of the unexpected, serve an unusual bread, salad, or your own special creation.

Squash and Swiss Cheese Casserole

(photograph on page 163)

HANDS-ON **1 HOUR, 5 MINUTES**   TOTAL **1 HOUR, 40 MINUTES**   SERVES **12**

There are so many recipes for squash casserole. This one is very refined and elegant. No "can of cream" shortcuts. I turn to this casserole when we are busting at the seams with squash. Make two or three at a time, freeze the ones you're not using, and in January when you are sick and tired of winter, you'll have a squash casserole to transport you back to those lazy summer days.

3 to 4 pounds yellow squash, cut into
⅓-inch slices (about 8 ½ cups)

2 medium-size yellow onions, chopped

2 bay leaves

6 flat-leaf parsley sprigs

2 thyme sprigs

½ cup (4 ounces) salted butter

6 tablespoons (about 1 ⅝ ounces)
all-purpose flour

3 cups whole milk

½ teaspoon kosher salt

1 teaspoon seasoned salt (such as Lawry's)

1 teaspoon Worcestershire sauce

⅛ teaspoon ground nutmeg

⅛ teaspoon cayenne pepper

4 large egg yolks, lightly beaten

6 ounces Swiss cheese, shredded
(about 1 ½ cups)

1 cup fresh breadcrumbs, from
1 baguette (about 2 ounces)

1   Preheat the oven to 350°F. Bring a large saucepan of salted water to a boil; add the squash, onions, bay leaves, parsley, and thyme. Cook until the squash is barely tender, about 10 minutes. Drain and discard the herbs.

2   While the squash cooks, melt 6 tablespoons of the butter in a medium saucepan over medium-high. Add the flour, and cook, whisking constantly, about 1 minute. Gradually whisk in the milk and cook, whisking constantly, until the mixture boils and thickens, about 11 minutes.

3   Remove from the heat, and whisk in the kosher salt, seasoned salt, Worcestershire sauce, nutmeg, and cayenne. Gradually stir about one-fourth of the hot milk mixture into the yolks; add the yolk mixture to the remaining hot milk mixture, stirring constantly.

4   Return the saucepan to medium-low; cook until slightly thickened, about 2 minutes. Whisk in 1 cup of the cheese. Add the sauce to the squash mixture; stir gently to combine. Pour into a lightly buttered broiler-proof 13- x 9-inch (3-quart) baking dish.

5   Melt the remaining butter; stir in the breadcrumbs. Sprinkle the breadcrumb mixture and remaining ¼ cup cheese over the squash. Bake until the top is lightly browned and the sauce is bubbly, about 35 minutes. Increase the oven temperature to broil. Broil 6 inches from the heat until the breadcrumbs are golden brown, about 2 to 3 minutes.

1972 SOUTHERN LIVING PARTY COOKBOOK ORIGINAL

Hoppin' John

HANDS-ON **10 MINUTES**   TOTAL **40 MINUTES**   SERVES **10**

Take care not to overcook the rice or the peas; the success of this dish depends on it. If it is overcooked, it will be a thick, gummy mess. If you're using dried peas, take the time to soak them overnight to ensure proper cooking time in relation to the rice.

4 bacon slices, chopped
¼ cup chopped yellow onion
   (from 1 onion)
3 cups water
1 ¼ teaspoons kosher salt

½ cup parboiled long-grain
   white rice (such as Uncle
   Ben's Original Converted)
4 cups frozen black-eyed peas
   (about 17 ½ ounces)
½ teaspoon black pepper
Sliced scallions (optional)

1 Heat a large saucepan over medium, and cook the bacon and onion, stirring occasionally, until the bacon is crisp and the onion is tender, about 8 minutes. Drain all but 1 tablespoon of the drippings; add 1 cup of the water and ¼ teaspoon of the salt to the pan, and bring to a boil over medium-high. Stir in the rice; cover, reduce the heat, and simmer until the rice is tender, about 18 minutes. Remove from the heat, and fluff with a fork.

2 Meanwhile, bring the remaining 2 cups of water to a boil in a medium saucepan over high. Add the peas and remaining 1 teaspoon salt; cover and simmer until the peas are tender, about 25 minutes. Drain the peas; stir the peas and black pepper into the rice mixture. Garnish with the scallions, if desired.

Banana Pudding Pie

HANDS-ON **20 MINUTES**   TOTAL **5 HOURS, 24 MINUTES,**
INCLUDING COOLING AND CHILLING TIME   SERVES **8**

Just when we thought there would never be anything more amazing than banana pudding, here comes this new kid on the block. Pull out your ripest bananas and put your diet on hold. This pie is destined to be a classic.

CRUST
1 (12-ounce) package vanilla wafers
½ cup (4 ounces) salted butter, melted
2 large bananas, sliced

VANILLA CREAM FILLING
¾ cup granulated sugar
⅓ cup (about 1 ½ ounces) all-purpose flour

2 large eggs
4 large egg yolks
2 cups whole milk
2 teaspoons vanilla extract

MERINGUE TOPPING
4 large egg whites
½ cup granulated sugar

1 Prepare the Crust: Preheat the oven to 350°F. Set aside 20 vanilla wafers; pulse the remaining vanilla wafers in a food processor 8 to 10 times or until coarsely crushed. (Should yield about 2 ½ cups.) Stir together the crushed vanilla wafers and butter until blended. Firmly press on the bottom and up the sides of a 9-inch pie plate.

2 Bake in the preheated oven for 10 to 12 minutes or until lightly browned. Remove to a wire rack, and let cool 30 minutes or until completely cool. Arrange the banana slices evenly over the bottom of the cooled crust.

3 Prepare the Vanilla Cream Filling: Whisk together the granulated sugar, flour, eggs, egg yolks, and milk in a heavy saucepan. Cook over medium-low heat, whisking constantly, 8 to 10 minutes or until it reaches the thickness of chilled pudding. (The mixture will just begin to bubble and will be thick enough to hold soft peaks when the whisk is lifted.) Remove from the heat, and stir in the vanilla.

4 Spread half of the hot filling over the bananas; top with the reserved 20 vanilla wafers. Spread the remaining hot filling over the vanilla wafers. (Filling will be about ¼ inch higher than the top edge of the crust.)

5 Prepare the Meringue Topping: Beat the egg whites with an electric mixer at high speed until foamy. Add the sugar, 1 tablespoon at a time, beating until stiff peaks form and the sugar dissolves. Spread the meringue evenly over the hot filling, sealing the edges.

6 Bake in the preheated oven for 10 to 12 minutes or until golden brown. Remove from the oven, and let cool 1 hour on a wire rack or until completely cool. Chill 4 hours.

CHRISTENING
BRUNCH

Crêpes St. Jacques

Casserole Baked Tomatoes

Basic Green Salad

Quick Petit Fours

CHRISTENING BRUNCH

We christened all three of my girls at the Grace Episcopal Church in Rosedale. I might have gone a little overboard. This was the first party I had for each of my daughters, and it was a foretelling of weddings to come. It's no secret I'm a little obsessed with weddings. Think about it: Both christenings and weddings start in a church, the girl wears a white gown, and there is a big celebration afterward with amazing food and flowers. Can you blame me for drawing parallels?

Although it will be a beautiful day, I won't deny that it will be a little stressful. Let me paint a picture: You are holding a newborn, you're sleep deprived and hormonal. To add injury to insult, you probably don't fit into your favorite church dress anymore. Now you're facing an important day you've planned to the last detail. My advice? Go into the day knowing that you need help. Not only do you have to get yourself ready at the crack of dawn, but you have to dress a newborn, clean your house, and set out a beautiful lunch. I cannot say this enough: Ask someone you love, who more important loves you back, for help. Otherwise, you won't get to enjoy your baby, your family, or this special day.

The key to the success of this party is to do as much as you can ahead of time. This menu is brilliant because it can be made well ahead. The only thing you need to do on the day of is toss the salad. Set out your buffet table, china, and glassware a week ahead. Set up your bar a few days ahead. The day before, call that sweet friend you enlisted and go over every detail with her. While you're at the church, your friend can heat up the food and fill the ice bucket on the bar so when you get back to the house, you are relaxed, can take pictures, and enjoy your family instead of sweating in the kitchen. I say this from experience. During my first child's christening, I was so worried about the food, the bar, making tea, and being sure my guests were taken care, that I didn't get a single photo holding my sweet baby girl after we left the church. I didn't see my daughter, Stott, the entire party. You can bet your life that I asked for help for my second child's christening. It was a whole other story.

Crêpes St. Jacques

HANDS-ON **1 HOUR**   TOTAL **2 HOURS, 10 MINUTES**   SERVES **8**

Crêpes take a little practice, but they are worth the effort. Lucy Mea Brown, the lady who helped raise me, made the best pancakes and crêpes you've ever had. She always said to plan on throwing the first two away because those are just to get you warmed up. The good news is that they freeze beautifully so make more than you need. Layer the crepês between parchment paper and freeze in an airtight container. A small nonstick 8-inch pan is critical for success.

CRÊPES
1 cup (about 4 ¼ ounces) all-purpose flour
⅔ cup whole milk
¼ teaspoon table salt
2 tablespoons unsalted butter, melted
2 large eggs, beaten
4 teaspoons vegetable oil

FILLING
2 tablespoons unsalted butter
¼ cup finely chopped yellow onion
   (from 1 onion)
2 garlic cloves, crushed
2 tablespoons all-purpose flour

1 cup Chablis wine (or use another
   dry white wine)
1 cup heavy cream
1 cup fresh lump crabmeat,
   drained and picked free of shell
1 cup chopped sea scallops
2 tablespoons fresh lemon juice
   (from 1 lemon)
1 teaspoon table salt
¼ teaspoon black pepper
Dash of Worcestershire sauce
Blender Hollandaise (page 186)
Chopped fresh flat-leaf parsley

1 Prepare the Crêpes: Process the flour, milk, salt, butter, and egg in a blender until the consistency of pancake batter, about 15 seconds. Chill 1 hour. Heat ½ teaspoon of the oil in an 8-inch nonstick skillet over medium-high. Pour about one-eighth (about 3 tablespoons) of the batter into the hot oil; swirl the batter to cover the bottom of the pan and make a very thin pancake. Cook until lightly browned underneath, about 30 seconds to 1 minute. Carefully loosen the edges of the crêpe with an offset spatula; flip and cook until lightly browned, about 30 seconds. Remove from the skillet; cover to keep warm. Repeat with the remaining oil and batter.

2 Prepare the Filling: Melt the butter in a medium saucepan over medium; add the onion and garlic, and cook, stirring constantly, 2 minutes. Add the flour; cook 1 minute. Stir in the wine and cream, and bring to a boil, stirring constantly. Cook until slightly thickened, about 1 minute. Stir in the crabmeat and scallops, and cook until the scallops are done, about 3 minutes. Remove from the heat, and stir in the lemon juice, salt, pepper, and Worcestershire sauce. Divide the mixture evenly among the crêpes, and roll up. Keep warm, if needed, in a 300°F oven for a few minutes. Serve warm with the Blender Hollandaise and sprinkled with chopped parsley .

Casserole Baked Tomatoes

(photograph on page 173)

HANDS-ON **20 MINUTES**   TOTAL **55 MINUTES**   SERVES **8**

McCarty's Pottery in Merigold is the crown jewel of Mississippi. They have a lovely tearoom that serves the most delightful lunches. One of the most popular dishes on the menu is the Merigold Tomatoes. This recipe is so guarded that at one time only two people knew it. I swear if this isn't the recipe Lee McCarty used then it is damn close. Fresh tomatoes are one of my favorite things on this planet, but not in the winter when tomatoes are mealy, hot, boxed, and come to the grocery from Timbuktu. This is a lovely way to get your tomato fix from a can.

2 tablespoons vegetable oil

1 small yellow onion, finely chopped (about 1 cup)

2 (28-ounce) cans whole tomatoes, drained and halved lengthwise

2 tablespoons light brown sugar

2 tablespoons chopped fresh chives

¾ teaspoon table salt

½ teaspoon seasoned salt (such as Lawry's)

½ teaspoon dried chervil

½ teaspoon dried dill

¼ teaspoon black pepper

1 cup coarse fresh breadcrumbs (from 1 baguette)

2 tablespoons salted butter, melted

1 Preheat the oven to 375°F. Heat the vegetable oil in a medium skillet over medium-high, and cook the onion until tender, about 6 minutes. Combine the onion, tomatoes, brown sugar, chives, table salt, seasoned salt, chervil, dill, and pepper in a medium bowl; pour into a lightly greased 2-quart baking dish.

2 Combine the breadcrumbs and the melted butter; sprinkle evenly over the top of the tomato mixture. Bake in the preheated oven until the breadcrumbs are golden, about 35 minutes.

Basic Green Salad

(photograph on page 173)

HANDS-ON **15 MINUTES**   TOTAL **15 MINUTES**   SERVES **8**

Every hostess needs the perfect black dress and every party needs the perfect green salad. This salad is simple, elegant, and understated. It's happy to let the other dishes take center stage.

One of the best investments one can make is a wooden salad bowl. There is an iconic restaurant in Greenville, Mississippi, called Doe's Eat Place, known for their porterhouse steaks. If you ask me, Miss Florence's salads are the star of the show at Doe's. Newlyweds can bring in their new wooden salad bowls and she'll make salads in them for a month or so to season their bowls properly.

¾ teaspoon table salt

1 small garlic clove

2 tablespoons extra-virgin olive oil

1 large head butter lettuce
  (about 7 ½ ounces)

¼ teaspoon black pepper

2 medium tomatoes, cut into
  8 wedges each

2 tablespoons red wine vinegar
  or fresh lemon juice

1 Place the salt and garlic in a large bowl. Use the back of a wooden spoon to mash the garlic and salt until the mixture is well blended and practically disappears. Discard any of the remaining solid pieces of garlic. Gradually press the oil into the garlic mixture with a spoon until well blended.

2 Tear the lettuce into bite-size pieces, and add to the garlic mixture in the bowl without tossing. (Prepare up to 1 hour before serving, and cover the bowl with a damp towel.)

3 Just before serving, sprinkle the greens with the pepper, and toss thoroughly until all of the greens are well coated with the oil. Add the tomatoes, and toss for a few seconds. Drizzle with the vinegar or lemon juice; toss and serve.

VARIATION: Mash the salt and garlic as directed above, adding 2 drained anchovies (or anchovy paste; mash into the salt. Add 1 teaspoon Dijon or Dusseldorf mustard and ⅛ teaspoon black pepper; continue to blend until the mixture forms a paste. Add 2 tablespoons extra-virgin olive oil and gradually press the oil into the garlic mixture with a spoon until blended. Gradually stir in 1 ½ tablespoons red wine vinegar or tarragon vinegar. Add the lettuce, toss well, and serve.

Quick Petits Fours

(photograph on page 170)

HANDS-ON **40 MINUTES**   TOTAL **1 HOUR, 40 MINUTES, INCLUDING FONDANT AND FROSTING**   SERVES **12**

Christening brunches and petits fours go together like white on rice. If the stress of having all of your family in town, cleaning the house, and caring for a newborn is too much, find a reputable bakery and order them. It's just like highlighting your hair; sometimes you need to hire someone or you may end up crying.

1 homemade or store-bought pound cake loaf (about 12 ounces)

2 tablespoons jam or jelly of choice

Petits Fours Fondant (recipe follows)

Decorative Frosting (recipe follows)

1 Trim the crust from the edges of the pound cake. Cut into ¾-inch-thick slices. Cut the slices into 24 (1 ½-inch) squares, or cut into shapes with small decorative cutters. Spread a small amount of jam or jelly (about ½ teaspoon) onto 1 side of 12 squares. Top with the remaining 12 squares.

2 Place the cakes on a wire rack placed over a rimmed baking sheet. Pour the Petits Fours Fondant over the cakes until completely coated, using a spoon or small measuring cup. Allow the cakes to dry completely on the rack, about 1 hour.

3 Spoon the Decorative Frosting into a pastry bag fitted with a piping tip. (Or use a large heavy-duty ziplock plastic bag and snip 1 corner.) Decorate the petits fours as desired.

Petits Fours Fondant

**6 ½ cups (about 26 ounces)
   powdered sugar, sifted**
½ cup water

2 tablespoons light corn syrup
⅛ teaspoon almond extract

Combine the powdered sugar, ½ cup water, and corn syrup in a medium saucepan. Cook over low until the sugar has dissolved and the mixture is smooth, about 4 minutes. Remove from the heat, and stir in the almond extract. **Makes 2 ¼ cups**

Decorative Frosting

**2 cups (about 8 ounces)
   powdered sugar, sifted**

**1 cup (8 ounces) unsalted
   butter, softened**

Beat the powdered sugar and butter with an electric mixer at medium speed until smooth, about 3 minutes. **Makes 1 cup**

Tip

There is no shame in picking up store-bought petits fours or cake bites. You can personalize them yourself with the Decorative Frosting or have the bakery do it for you.

Easter

Shrimp Rémoulade

Roast Leg of Lamb
Potatoes Gruyère
Spring Asparagus with Blender Hollandaise

Meringues

EASTER

Easter is and always has been one of my favorite holidays. After a long, cold, and dreary winter, Easter is a breath of fresh air and sunshine. I have such fun memories of the Easters of my childhood. We dyed all of the Easter eggs and left them out for the Easter Bunny. Mama and Daddy hid them before we woke up. One year we had a huge black lab that was just terrible. Mama and Daddy let him out before we woke up, and that dog sniffed out and ate all of the eggs and left pastel shell carcasses all over the yard. We were horrified as we ran out of the house in our nightgowns and bare feet with our baskets in hand. That same Easter, we found a nest of baby bunnies as we were finishing Easter brunch. Everyone gathered on the back porch to see them and "ooh" and "aah". Mama gently picked up one of the bunnies so the children could see better, and as she stood up, Cocoa, that terrible lab, snatched the baby bunny out of her hand and took off with it. No Easter Bunny cake or meringue dessert could erase that horror.

I've made sure Easter is festive and happy since the day it was tainted by Cocoa. One year, Amanda and I borrowed a page from Greg at the Garden District's playbook. We wanted to have an Easter egg hunt to beat all and a planted table, so I cut a piece of vinyl to the exact size of my table. I took it outside, spread it on the lawn, and covered it in a thin layer of potting soil. I sprinkled a thick layer of wheat grass seed on top, watered it, and waited. The grass grew, bright green and perfect. The day before Easter, I spread my tablecloth lawn on the dining table. I "planted" tulips and daffodils in small chunks of oasis hidden in the grass. I used all of my white platters and placed them directly on the grass. For a finishing touch, I added dyed Easter eggs to make the table even more festive. (You can get the same look with less trouble by just "growing" a small runner.) That year there were "oohs" and "aahs" at Easter again. Thankfully, minus the horror.

Shrimp Rémoulade

HANDS-ON **15 MINUTES**   TOTAL **15 MINUTES**   SERVES **8**

This is the perfect first course on ice on a buffet or plated individually. In New Orleans it is typically served on a bed of shredded iceberg lettuce. To me, that is like putting a king on a ripped-up mattress in a flop house. Please, if you're going to serve this plated on lettuce, do your guests a favor and put the shrimp rémoulade in butter lettuce cups. Now that's a presentation fit for royalty.

¼ cup mayonnaise

1 bunch scallions, sliced

⅓ cup chopped fresh parsley

2 tablespoons prepared horseradish

2 tablespoons Creole mustard

2 tablespoons Dijon mustard

1 tablespoon fresh lemon juice (from 1 lemon)

2 pounds peeled cooked shrimp

Butter lettuce leaves (optional)

Lemon wedges

Stir together the mayonnaise, scallions, parsley, horseradish, Creole mustard, Dijon mustard, and lemon juice. Cover and chill until ready to serve. Serve the shrimp in butter lettuce leaves, if desired, with the sauce and lemon wedges on the side.

PARTY RULE NO. 6

No one should hold 'em

Always include a dish for pits, tails, shells, or wooden picks (or you may find them stashed in plants, between couch cushions, or in votive holders for weeks to come). Be sure it's easy for guests to differentiate fresh wooden picks from discarded ones.

Roast Leg of Lamb

HANDS-ON 50 MINUTES TOTAL **10 HOURS, 40 MINUTES**
INCLUDING 8 HOURS CHILLING TIME SERVES **8 TO 10**

My mother was a master of leg of lamb. She grilled it on a charcoal grill. I can still remember her standing in the garage on Sunday after church in her heels, pearls, and perfect hair. Using an enormous fork, she lifted what looked like a dinosaur drumstick off the grill. The look of satisfaction on her face was priceless. She had entered a man's world and conquered it.

Roasting the leg of lamb in an oven makes it a little less intimidating. This is the only recipe I have ever seen that uses an olive to trap the marinade in each slit cut into the lamb. It's sheer genius. If cooking lamb scares you, pretend that it's a chuck roast. See, now don't you feel better?

1 (6-pound) bone-in leg of lamb,
   trimmed
1 tablespoon paprika
2 teaspoons seasoned salt
   (such as Lawry's)
1 teaspoon dried oregano
1 teaspoon black pepper
½ teaspoon ground ginger

½ teaspoon dry mustard
1 ½ teaspoons kosher salt
¼ cup fresh lime juice (from 2 limes)
2 garlic cloves, crushed
½ teaspoon dried marjoram
3 or 4 dashes of hot sauce (such as Tabasco)
20 pimiento-stuffed green olives
Oregano sprigs (optional)

1 Place the lamb in a large roasting pan. Combine the paprika, seasoned salt, oregano, pepper, ginger, mustard, and 1 teaspoon of the kosher salt; rub the mixture evenly over the lamb on all sides.

2 Stir together the lime juice, garlic, marjoram, hot sauce, and remaining ½ teaspoon kosher salt in a small bowl. Using a paring knife, cut 20 holes (¾ inch wide x ¾ inch deep) in the meaty side of the lamb. Pour a little of the lime juice mixture into each hole, and insert a stuffed olive, like a stopper. Cover and chill 8 hours or overnight. Reserve and chill any remaining lime juice mixture for basting.

3 Preheat the oven to 350°F. Remove the lamb from the refrigerator; uncover. Bake in the preheated oven until a thermometer inserted in the thickest portion registers 130°F, about 1 hour and 30 minutes, basting with the remaining lime juice mixture every 30 minutes. Remove from the oven, and let stand 20 minutes before slicing.

VARIATION: Season the lamb as desired (with dry seasonings), and grate 1 green apple and 1 onion over the top. Bake slowly, basting with dry sherry during cooking.

Note

If desired, skim the fat from the drippings in the pan;
add enough hot water to make a rich gravy.

1972 SOUTHERN LIVING PARTY COOKBOOK ORIGINAL

Potatoes Gruyère

HANDS-ON **20 MINUTES**   TOTAL **1 HOUR, 30 MINUTES**   SERVES **8**

Gruyère is a type of Swiss cheese with a nutty flavor. It is much stronger in taste and smell than the Swiss cheese you get at the corner Piggly Wiggly. Since this dish has so few ingredients, do spring for the fairly expensive Gruyère to make it Easter-worthy.

¼ cup (2 ounces) salted butter, melted, plus more softened butter for greasing

5 medium-size russet potatoes (about 3 pounds total), peeled and cut into ⅛-inch-thick slices

1 ¼ teaspoons kosher salt

½ teaspoon black pepper

5 cups beef broth

4 ounces Gruyère cheese, shredded (about 1 cup)

1 Preheat the oven to 350°F. Generously butter a 3-quart baking dish. Place one-third of the potato slices in a single layer in the prepared dish; drizzle with one-third of the melted butter, and sprinkle with one-third of the salt and one-third of the pepper. Repeat the layers of the potatoes, butter, salt, and pepper twice. Pour in enough broth to cover the potatoes well; reserve any remaining broth for another use.

2 Bake, uncovered, in the preheated oven until tender throughout, about 1 hour. Use a small sharp knife to check for doneness. Remove from the oven, and drain off any excess liquid. Sprinkle with the cheese, and return to the oven. Bake until the cheese is golden brown, about 10 minutes.

Spring Asparagus with Blender Hollandaise

(photograph on page 185)

HANDS-ON **10 MINUTES**   TOTAL **20 MINUTES**   SERVES **8**

Hollandaise must be made at the last minute, which can cause a major problem for a host or hostess. Your guests have arrived, and you're making sure everyone has been welcomed and is enjoying a drink and hors d'oeuvre. You are trying to be engaging and lovely while maintaining perfect posture and keeping lipstick on. The last thing you need to do is dart into the kitchen and start frantically whisking a bunch of egg yolks over the stove. God forbid you lose focus and curdle the precious egg yolks, and then you are back to square one.

Enter the savior of the party: the fail-proof blender hollandaise. It's the best thing since sliced bread. You can keep it warm over hot water or pour it into an insulated cup or thermos.

2 pounds fresh asparagus, trimmed

3 large pasteurized egg yolks

2 tablespoons fresh lemon juice (from 1 lemon)

¼ teaspoon table salt

Dash of cayenne pepper

⅔ cup (5 ⅓ ounces) unsalted butter

1 Fill a large saucepan with 1 inch of water; bring to a boil over medium-high. Place the asparagus, trimmed sides down, in batches if needed, in a steamer basket in the boiling water, and steam until crisp-tender, about 4 to 5 minutes.

2 Meanwhile, combine the egg yolks, lemon juice, salt, and cayenne pepper in a blender. Cover and process on high speed for 3 seconds. (Do not remove the mixture from the blender.)

3 Heat the butter in a small saucepan over medium until it bubbles. Remove the center piece of the blender lid. With the blender running on high speed, slowly pour the melted butter into the blender, and continue to blend until smooth and thickened. Immediately drizzle over the asparagus, or keep warm until ready to serve.

Meringues with Fresh Strawberries and Chantilly Cream

HANDS-ON **15 MINUTES**   TOTAL **9 HOURS, 30 MINUTES,**
INCLUDING DRYING TIME   SERVES **8**

This recipe makes rectangle meringues, which is a nice presentation for a buffet or a luncheon. My grandmother always made them in circles that were the perfect size for a dessert plate, and this is the recipe she has always made for Easter. It's been this way for 70 years, and I don't see it changing anytime soon. Some things are too good to change.

4 large egg whites

½ teaspoon cream of tartar

½ cup granulated sugar

1 (8-ounce) container crème fraîche
   or sour cream

¾ cup whipping cream

¾ teaspoon vanilla extract

3 tablespoons powdered sugar

1 quart fresh strawberries,
   hulled and sliced

1 Preheat the oven to 250°F. Cover a large baking sheet with parchment paper. Trace the bottom of a 9- x 5-inch loaf pan on paper twice. Turn the paper over; secure with masking tape.

2 Beat the egg whites and cream of tartar with an electric mixer at high speed until foamy. Add the granulated sugar, 1 tablespoon at a time, beating until stiff peaks form and the sugar dissolves. Using a small spatula, spread half of the meringue 1 inch thick onto each drawn rectangle to completely fill the rectangles. Bake in the preheated oven for 1 hour and 15 minutes. Turn the oven off, and let the meringues stand in the closed oven overnight.

3 Beat the crème fraîche in a large bowl with an electric mixer at medium speed 30 seconds. Add the whipping cream, vanilla, and powdered sugar; beat at high speed 3 minutes or until soft peaks form.

4 To assemble, remove the meringues from the parchment paper onto a serving platter. Top each evenly with strawberries and cream.

Tip

Trace the rectangles on the side
of parchment paper that curls up. When
you turn the paper over, it will lie flat
on the baking sheet without having to
secure it with tape.

Make Perfect Golden Eggs

1

START WITH 24 EGGS, hard cooked or wooden craft store eggs. Create a drying rack by inserting wooden picks into plastic foam.

2

APPLY ADHESIVE ALL OVER EACH EGG with a foam brush. Then let dry on the rack for about 30 minutes.

3

TEAR OFF A SHEET OF GOLD FOIL. Place an egg in the center of the sheet, and cover with the foil.

4

GENTLY RUB OFF ANY EXCESS or bumpy gold foil with cheesecloth. Save these foil pieces for additional eggs.

5

ONCE THE EGG IS COVERED, APPLY SEALER all over it with another foam brush. Repeat the process with other eggs.

6

PLACE ON THE DRYING RACK for at least an hour to let the foil set completely before handling the egg.

189

garden
club luncheon

Vichyssoise
Puff Pastry Chicken Salad Ring
Cranberry-Strawberry Salad
Marinated Vegetable Salad
Peach Melba

GARDEN CLUB LUNCHEON

I have been so lucky and honored to speak at garden clubs all over the South. Once you get asked to speak at one, it's like your name suddenly gets put on a "Do-call List" sent to all the other clubs in surrounding communities, and next thing you know, you are on the garden club-speaking circuit. Let me tell you one thing, it is a good circuit to be on. I get to dress up and act like a lady for a day as opposed to my normal day of running around in stretch pants with no makeup on in a hot kitchen.

The best part of any garden club meeting is the lunch. I have been to hundreds of garden club luncheons, and I can honestly tell you that I have yet to be disappointed. Typically, there is a committee that oversees the planning and executing of the luncheon. These women are intent on impressing their peers and I get to reap the benefits. I get so excited about great food that I didn't have to cook that I often end up eating way too fast and way too much. See, we don't stop to eat lunch in my catering kitchen because there's never time. Plus, the last thing you want to do is eat when you're cooking all day. So I forget my manners when I actually get to sit down and eat off a plate with a group of lovely ladies. I truly am trying to work on it so cut me some slack.

Most of these ladies have been in garden clubs and other social clubs for years, so they've had every kind of chicken salad known to man. You must think outside the box to impress them, though it's not a bad idea to pull an old favorite from the recipe box that's accumulated a little dust, or find one in an old community cookbook that has meaning to you. It's nice for a recipe to have some history so you can share it over lunch. Always select recipes that are easy to make so that the ladies on the committee can have success and impress.

Vichyssoise

HANDS-ON **35 MINUTES**   TOTAL **4 HOURS, 30 MINUTES**   SERVES **8**

Why is it that when a recipe name is French I feel fear welling up in the pit of my stomach? Cold potato soup is not scary. Vichyssoise SOUNDS scary. Yet my fear was completely unfounded because this soup is a breeze to make.

One of the most perfect parties I've attended was in Sumner, Mississippi, at the home of Julia Turnipseed. All of the guests were invited outside into the magnificent gardens where vichyssoise appeared in front of us in dainty demitasse cups on silver platters. The soup was garnished with snipped chives and the tiniest piece of bacon. Every time I make this soup I am transported back to that lovely party.

2 tablespoons salted butter

4 small leeks or scallions (about 11 ounces), trimmed, washed, and thinly sliced

1 small yellow onion, thinly sliced (about ¾ cup)

5 medium-size russet potatoes (about 3 ¼ pounds), peeled and thinly sliced

4 cups chicken broth

1 cup water

½ teaspoon kosher salt

⅛ teaspoon cayenne pepper

3 cups whipping cream

Chopped fresh chives and cracked black pepper

1 Melt the butter in a large Dutch oven over medium. Add the leeks and onion, and cook, stirring often, until almost tender, about 9 minutes. Stir in the potatoes, broth, 1 cup water, salt, and cayenne pepper; bring to a boil. Cover, reduce the heat to low, and simmer gently until the vegetables are tender, about 45 minutes. Remove from the heat, and cool 10 minutes.

2 Pour the mixture into a food processor, in batches if needed, and process until smooth, about 2 to 3 minutes. Return to the Dutch oven; stir in the cream. Cover and refrigerate until thoroughly chilled, about 3 hours. Garnish each serving with the chopped chives and cracked black pepper.

Puff Pastry Chicken Salad Ring

HANDS-ON **30 MINUTES**   TOTAL **1 HOUR, 20 MINUTES**   SERVES **8**

This recipe only looks daunting, but I promise it is worth the effort. This recipe was given to me by my good friend Stephanie. She loves to serve this at ladies luncheons and late brunches. Just one more way to make chicken salad. Are we at 1,000 ways yet?

2 cups shredded cooked deli-
   roasted chicken

4 ounces Swiss cheese, shredded
   (about 1 cup)

½ cup mayonnaise

½ cup finely chopped celery
   (from 1 large stalk)

½ cup golden raisins

¼ cup chopped toasted walnuts

1 teaspoon Greek seasoning
   (such as Cavender's)

½ (17.3-ounce) package frozen
   puff pastry sheets, thawed

1 large egg white, lightly beaten

1   Preheat the oven to 375°F. Combine the chicken, cheese, mayonnaise, celery, raisins, walnuts, and Greek seasoning in a medium bowl.

2   Roll the puff pastry into a 13- x 11-inch rectangle on a lightly floured surface; spread with the chicken mixture, leaving a ½-inch border. Roll up from 1 long side; pinch the long edges to seal. Bring the ends together to form into a 7-inch ring, and pinch the ends to seal. Place on a baking sheet lined with parchment paper. Brush lightly with the egg white.

3   Bake in the preheated oven until puffed, golden brown, and cooked throughout, about 40 minutes. Cool 10 minutes before serving. Cut into 8 wedges.

Cranberry-Strawberry Salad

HANDS-ON **20 MINUTES** TOTAL **8 HOURS, 50 MINUTES,
INCLUDING CHILLING TIME** SERVES **12**

Marilyn Ragan was one of my favorite people on this earth. She was like a second mother to me, and she liked me almost as much as she liked congealed salads. When I started catering, she hired me to help her entertain but would always provide the recipe. I made a recipe similar to this one, following her recipe to a T. When I took it to her she said, "Well, this isn't it." I made it again and, again, she said, "It's not right." To which I replied, "Okay, you make it and let me watch so I can see what I am doing wrong." Marilyn said, "You know, I'm no cook. I just know what it's supposed to look like, and this is not it."

I wish I knew how many packages of gelatin were consumed in the South compared to the North. I would have to guess at least two to one. There's hardly an occasion where a congealed salad isn't a welcome guest.

1 ½ cups fresh or frozen cranberries

2 cups diced fresh strawberries

½ cup granulated sugar

2 cups boiling water

3 (3-ounce) packages strawberry gelatin

2 cups cranberry juice, chilled

1 (8-ounce) can crushed pineapple, undrained

1 cup diced celery

Lettuce leaves (optional)

Fresh berries (optional)

1 Process the cranberries in a food processor 30 seconds or until coarsely chopped, stopping once to scrape down the sides. Stir together the cranberries, strawberries, and sugar in a medium bowl.

2 Combine 2 cups boiling water and the gelatin in a large bowl, stirring 2 minutes or until the gelatin dissolves. Stir in the juice, and chill 30 minutes or until the mixture is the consistency of unbeaten egg whites.

3 Stir in the cranberry mixture, pineapple, and celery. Spoon the mixture into 12 lightly greased (⅔-cup) molds or custard cups; cover and chill 8 hours or until firm. To serve, gently run a knife around the edges of each mold. Turn out onto serving plates lined with lettuce leaves, if desired. Garnish with fresh berries, if desired.

PARTY RULE NO. 7

Make light of party fouls

Downplay spills. Treat them immediately, but deal with them later. Dab tomato-based spills with a bit of liquid dish soap. White vinegar treats juice, coffee, and tea stains. Neutralize red wine stains with white wine and then a layer of salt. Cover treated spills with a towel. After guests depart, blot and rinse the stain with distilled white vinegar and rinse with cool water or club soda.

Marinated Veggie (Lots of Veggies) Salad

HANDS-ON **15 MINUTES**   TOTAL **8 HOURS, 15 MINUTES,**
INCLUDING MARINATING TIME   SERVES **8**

Feel free to use your favorite combination of vegetables in this recipe, but remember to include lots of color. My favorite combination is blanched asparagus, multicolored peppers, cucumbers, green beans, and cherry tomatoes. The vegetables can be blanched and chopped a day ahead. Add the marinade about two to four hours before serving so the veggies can fully absorb the wonderful dressing.

8 ounces fresh green beans

1 (15-ounce) can chickpeas (garbanzo beans), drained and rinsed

1 cup halved cherry tomatoes (from 1 pint)

3/4 cup thinly diagonally sliced celery (from 2 stalks)

3/4 cup thinly sliced red onion (from 1 small onion)

3 tablespoons sherry vinegar

1 tablespoon honey

1 teaspoon Dijon mustard

1 teaspoon kosher salt

3/4 teaspoon black pepper

6 tablespoons olive oil

1/4 cup chopped fresh basil

1 teaspoon chopped fresh thyme

1 Fill a medium bowl with ice and water. Bring a pot of salted water to a boil over high. Add the green beans, and cook until crisp-tender and bright green, about 4 minutes. Plunge into the ice water using a slotted spoon or tongs. Let stand until thoroughly chilled, about 5 minutes. Remove the green beans, and pat dry with a paper towel. Cut into 1-inch pieces, and place in a large bowl.

2 Add the chickpeas, tomatoes, celery, and red onion to the bowl with the green beans. Set aside while you prepare the vinaigrette.

3 Whisk together the vinegar, honey, mustard, salt, and pepper in a small bowl. Slowly drizzle in the oil, whisking constantly, until emulsified. Drizzle the vinaigrette over the vegetables, and toss to coat. Cover and chill until the onions are tender and the vegetables are flavorful, at least 8 hours and up to 24 hours, tossing occasionally. Toss with the basil and thyme just before serving. Serve the salad chilled or at room temperature.

Peach Melba

HANDS-ON 15 MINUTES TOTAL 15 MINUTES SERVES 8

This dish was created in 1892 by French chef Auguste Escoffier at the Savoy Hotel in London to honor Australian opera singer Nellie Melba. There is a reason that this dessert has remained popular for more than 100 years. It's simply delicious. Be sure that the peaches are at the peak of ripeness. Whenever you have a recipe that has this few ingredients, each one needs to be perfect.

½ cup seedless raspberry jam

2 tablespoons (1 ounce) peach brandy

1 quart vanilla ice cream

4 medium-size fresh peaches,
    peeled, pitted, and quartered

⅔ cup whipping cream

2 tablespoons granulated sugar

Mint leaves (optional)

Fresh raspberries (optional)

Gaufrette wafer cookies or
    other cookies

1 Stir together the jam and brandy in a small bowl until pouring consistency. Scoop ¼ cup of the ice cream into each of 8 cocktail glasses or dessert dishes. Top each with 2 peach quarters, and drizzle with 1 tablespoon jam mixture.

2 Beat the cream and sugar with an electric mixer at high speed until soft peaks form, about 1 minute. Top each serving with a dollop of whipped cream. Garnish with mint leaves and a few fresh raspberries, if desired. Serve with the gaufrettes.

salad
salad
salad

Sea Island Shrimp

Curried Chicken Salad

Lemony Green Bean Pasta Salad

Whole Wheat Finger Sandwiches
with Olive Spread

Frozen Lemon Cream

SALAD, SALAD, SALAD

The Salad, Salad, Salad luncheon gives you a no-stress, excuse-free opportunity to invite your friends over to reconnect and reminisce. Anytime I sit down for lunch at a restaurant with a cold salad plate on the menu, you can bet a dollar that is what I am ordering. I love it for lots of reasons, but the number one reason is that you get a lot of variety on your plate. It is so hard for me to make a decision when I look at a menu because I. want. it. all! With a salad plate you usually get three different choices on one plate, which ensures that I won't have order-envy if my lunch date orders better than me. I think it must be the reason that we turn to the cold salad plate for so many of our catered luncheons. We love to serve one of the salads in a butter lettuce cup. It's just like our mothers and grandmothers did with the iceberg lettuce leaf, only a bit fresher and a lot prettier. I like to put the other salad in a toast cup or pastry shell. Purple radicchio and pale green endive leaves are great options for the last salad.

Then we get to my other favorite thing—the finger sandwich. Finger sandwich options are endless, but pimiento, cucumber, egg salad, and olive spread are at the top of my list. If finger sandwiches don't float your boat, then a ham biscuit or sweet muffin is a hearty addition to the salad, salad, salad plate. Remember that all of these salads can be prepared days ahead, making this menu ideal when your schedule is packed, but you still want to have the girls over for lunch. Include a basket of artisan breads or crackers on the table for those friends who aren't carb-phobic, and keep dessert light and simple. A frozen dessert is lovely and echoes our favorite phrase in the English language: "Can be made ahead and freezes beautifully."

Sea Island Shrimp

HANDS-ON **20 MINUTES**   TOTAL **8 HOURS, 20 MINUTES,
INCLUDING CHILLING TIME**   SERVES **8**

"Prepare the day before" is music to an overwhelmed hostess' ears. Recipes that can be made the day before are the hallmark of a successful party. Trust me, on the day of the party you have furniture to dust, monogrammed towels to put out, and husbands to yell at.

1 ⅓ cups extra-virgin olive oil

⅔ cup tarragon vinegar

¾ cup fresh lemon juice
   (from 2 lemons)

2 teaspoons kosher salt

½ teaspoon black pepper

3 quarts water

2 pounds large peeled, deveined raw
   shrimp

1 lemon, very thinly sliced

1 small yellow onion, very thinly sliced
   (about 1 ½ cups sliced)

Wooden picks

1 Whisk together the oil, vinegar, lemon juice, salt, and pepper in a large bowl until combined; set aside.

2 Bring 3 quarts water to a boil in a large saucepan over high. Add the shrimp; cook until almost done, about 3 minutes. Drain the shrimp, and add immediately to the oil mixture. Add the sliced lemon and onion; toss to coat. Cover and refrigerate 8 hours or overnight. Serve the shrimp in the marinade with wooden picks.

salad
salad
salad

Sea Island Shrimp
Curried Chicken Salad
Lemony Green Bean Pasta Salad
Whole Wheat Finger Sandwiches
with Olive Spread

Curried Chicken Salad

HANDS-ON **15 MINUTES** TOTAL **3 HOURS, 20 MINUTES,**
INCLUDING CHILLING TIME SERVES **8**

I've loved hot curry chicken since I was a child. I had the honor of being asked to be a Godmother to Mary Helen Quinn. At the christening, Mary Helen's mother served chicken curry. I cannot tell you whether it's the curry flavor or all the mix-ins that are my favorite part of this dish. You don't have to choose all the toppings for this cold curried chicken salad; they are mixed in for you.

$\frac{1}{2}$ cup mayonnaise

$\frac{1}{2}$ cup sour cream

$\frac{1}{4}$ cup finely chopped scallions

1 tablespoon grated fresh ginger

2 teaspoons curry powder

4 cups diced cooked chicken

1 cup diced celery

$\frac{3}{4}$ cup golden raisins

$\frac{3}{4}$ cup diced yellow bell pepper

$\frac{3}{4}$ cup toasted sweetened flaked
  coconut

$\frac{1}{2}$ cup chopped lightly salted
  roasted peanuts

1 Whisk together the mayonnaise and sour cream in a large bowl; add the scallions, ginger, and curry powder to the mayonnaise mixture, and whisk to combine. Stir in the chicken and celery.

2 Stir the golden raisins and bell pepper into the chicken mixture. Add salt and pepper to taste. Chill 3 hours. Stir in the coconut, and top with the peanuts just before serving.

Lemony Green Bean Pasta Salad

HANDS-ON **15 MINUTES**   TOTAL **30 MINUTES**   SERVES **8**

Some pasta salads are so heavy and mayonnaise-laden that they elicit the gag reflex. This pasta salad, however, is light and extremely fresh. Add chicken or shrimp on top for a quick and easy supper.

12 ounces casarecce (or penne) pasta

8 ounces haricots verts (French green beans), cut in half lengthwise

1 tablespoon fresh thyme leaves

5 teaspoons lemon zest (from 2 lemons)

¼ cup finely chopped roasted salted pistachios, plus more for garnish

2 tablespoons Champagne vinegar

1 tablespoon minced shallots

1 garlic clove, minced

1 teaspoon table salt

½ teaspoon freshly ground black pepper

5 tablespoons olive oil

1 ½ cups loosely packed arugula

Grated Parmesan cheese

1 Cook the pasta according to the package directions, adding the green beans to the boiling water during the last 2 minutes of cooking time; drain. Rinse the pasta and green beans with cold water; drain well.

2 Place the pasta mixture, thyme, and 3 teaspoons of the lemon zest in a large bowl; toss gently to combine.

3 Whisk together ¼ cup pistachios, vinegar, shallots, garlic, salt, pepper, and the remaining 2 teaspoons lemon zest in a small bowl. Add the oil in a slow, steady stream, whisking constantly until blended. Drizzle over the pasta mixture. Add the arugula, and toss gently to coat. Garnish with the chopped pistachios and Parmesan cheese.

Finger Sandwiches with Olive Spread

HANDS-ON **10 MINUTES**   TOTAL **10 MINUTES**   SERVES **16**

This olive spread has been a staple for gatherings at my husband's family's lake house in Herber Springs, Arkansas, for years. Some lake days we are too lazy to even make a sandwich. That's when we eat the olive spread right out of the container with a saltine cracker.

½ cup slivered almonds (or use chopped pecans), finely chopped

1 (4 ½-ounce) can chopped black olives

½ teaspoon Worcestershire sauce

Seasoned salt to taste

Lemon juice to taste

2 to 3 teaspoons favorite vinaigrette

Mayonnaise

½ (16-ounce) loaf sliced whole-wheat sandwich bread

½ (16-ounce) loaf sliced white sandwich bread

1 Stir together the almonds, olives, Worcestershire sauce, seasoned salt, lemon juice, vinaigrette, and enough mayonnaise to reach a spreading consistency in a small bowl.

2 Trim the crusts from the bread. Spread the olive mixture evenly on 1 side of half of the bread slices; top with remaining bread slices. Cut each sandwich diagonally into 2 triangles.

PARTY RULE NO. 8

Make ahead…but keep it fresh

Make-ahead recipes are a host's best friend. The key is to be sure a dish tastes freshly made when it's served. Tiny finger sandwiches are big on flavor. Most can be prepared up to a day ahead and refrigerated in an airtight container. Prevent the bread from drying out by covering the sandwiches with a sheet of wax paper and top with a damp paper towel. Uncover the sandwiches just before you are ready to serve and the bread will be pillowy soft. Keep freshness AND convenience in mind!

Frozen Lemon Cream

HANDS-ON **10 MINUTES**   TOTAL **6 HOURS, 10 MINUTES,**
INCLUDING FREEZING TIME   SERVES **12**

A light lemon dessert is a delightful way to end a luncheon. This is a simple recipe that produces great results, and there's no need for an ice-cream maker or boxes of rock salt.

2 cups granulated sugar

2 cups whole milk

2 cups heavy cream

¼ teaspoon table salt

3 tablespoons lemon zest, plus ²/₃ cup fresh juice (from about 4 lemons)

1 Combine the sugar, milk, cream, and salt in a medium saucepan, and heat over medium, stirring constantly, just until the sugar is dissolved, about 6 minutes. (Don't allow the mixture to boil.) Pour into a 1¼- to 2-quart baking dish, and freeze until firm, about 3 hours.

2 Scoop the frozen mixture into the bowl of an electric stand mixer; beat at medium speed until smooth and creamy, about 2 minutes, gradually adding the lemon zest and juice.

3 Return the mixture to the baking dish, and freeze just until almost firm, about 1 hour. Using a fork, vigorously stir the mixture in the dish until smooth, about 1 minute. Cover and freeze until firm, about 2 hours.

Note

An attractive way to serve this dessert is to cut small oranges in half, scoop out the pulp, fill with the frozen lemon cream, and freeze in the cups. A twisted citrus slice perched on top of the dessert is a nice touch.

Cookouts

If you are new to entertaining (or just old and tired), a cookout is the ideal party to host! Just the mention of "cookout" evokes visions of good ole relaxing, laid-back fun. Beautiful weather is often short-lived, so take advantage of those comfortable sunny days in the South. For this easy outdoor gathering, there is no need to scrub the house from top to bottom or break your budget on decor. Mother Nature has already done her magic! Don't detract from all that natural beauty with a bunch of knickknacks and sit-arounds. Do sweep the patio, wipe the pollen off of the chairs, and rake the leaves, but don't fret spills or stress over seating charts. This is as easy as it gets. Best of all, food always tastes better when it is served outside!

Backyard BBQ

BARBECUED CHICKEN

MARINATED HERBED TOMATOES | SIDNEY'S POTATO SALAD

CHEWY BROWNIE ICE-CREAM SANDWICHES

BACKYARD BBQ

When the weather is beautiful, there is hardly any place I would rather be than outside. I just love to have my friends over for a backyard barbecue.

Divide and conquer for this casual party and enlist the help of your whole family. Let your husband man the grill. Over the years I've noticed that if men learn that they will get to play with fire, they are much more likely to lend a hand. I say "let 'em!" Why in the world would you want to be standing next to a hot grill in the middle of the summer with your eyes watering from the smoke? Involve the kids too. They are great for helping with the dessert. I'm a big believer in letting children see that getting ready for the party can be just as much fun as the actual main event. Plus, kids are really expensive, so I consider putting them to work a good way for them to give back. Child labor laws do not apply at my house.

There is something magical about sitting under the stars after a wonderful meal that evokes the most amazing conversations. So, I say get creative and set up everything outside—from tables and chairs to the buffet. One of the best buffet setups we ever used wasn't a table at all. We placed a chippy, old, painted door on top of two sawhorses and it was perfect. . .I didn't fret over barbecue sauce spills, cup rings, or puddles of melted ice cream on the surface either.

Keep in mind that if you want your guests to relax after dinner, enjoy the music, and have fun conversations filled with laughter—keep your butt in the chair instead of cleaning up! My friends who are reading this are rolling their eyes at me because this is the hardest thing for me to do. As soon as guests finish eating, I am the first to hop up and start clearing the plates and platters, wrapping up all the leftovers, and washing dishes. I should practice what I preach because this really is the worst party foul one can commit. It makes your guests feel uncomfortable and compelled to work or take their leave. Keep that in mind. If you are ready for guests to depart, the party is over, or someone has overstayed their welcome, then by all means get out the dust buster and let the cleaning begin.

Barbecued Chicken

HANDS-ON 1 HOUR, 30 MINUTES   TOTAL 5 HOURS, 30 MINUTES, INCLUDING 4 HOURS CHILLING   SERVES 8

Grilling chicken sounds easy enough, but the first time I made BBQ chicken it turned out black and charred beyond recognition on the outside and raw as sashimi on the inside. Not the result you are hoping for when you've got a houseful of hungry guests. Remember: Your coals need to go from fire engine red to grey ash before you start grilling. It takes a bit of patience to get there, but when the chicken comes off perfect coals, you will be fielding the praise of your guests instead of ordering delivery pizzas.

2 (4-pound) whole chickens

BRINE
1 ¼ cups apple cider vinegar
½ cup fresh lemon juice
   (from about 3 lemons)
2 ½ tablespoons ketchup
2 ¼ teaspoons yellow mustard
1 ½ teaspoons table salt
½ teaspoon black pepper

BROWNING SAUCE
¼ cup (2 ounces) salted butter, melted
3 tablespoons granulated sugar
2 tablespoons yellow mustard
1 ½ teaspoons Worcestershire sauce
½ teaspoon table salt
¼ teaspoon black pepper

1 Use kitchen shears to remove the backbones from the chickens and then quarter each chicken into 2 breast halves and 2 whole legs (thighs with drumsticks attached).

2 Prepare the Brine: Whisk together the apple cider vinegar, lemon juice, ketchup, mustard, salt, and pepper in a large bowl. Divide the brine between 2 (1-gallon) heavy-duty ziplock plastic freezer bags. Place 4 chicken quarters in each bag. Seal the bags and chill 4 to 8 hours, turning the bags occasionally.

3 Prepare the Browning Sauce: Whisk together the melted butter, sugar, mustard, Worcestershire sauce, salt, and pepper in a saucepan. Simmer over medium-low, stirring often, until the sugar is melted. Reserve about ¼ cup Browning Sauce.

4 Preheat the grill to medium-low (300° to 350°F). Remove the chicken from the marinade, and discard the marinade. Place the chicken on oiled grates. Grill, uncovered, until the chicken is cooked through, turning and basting occasionally with the remaining Browning Sauce, about 55 minutes. Discard any remaining Browning Sauce used to baste the chicken. Reheat the reserved ¼ cup Browning Sauce to serve with the chicken.

1972 SOUTHERN LIVING PARTY COOKBOOK ORIGINAL

Marinated Herbed Tomatoes

HANDS-ON **30 MINUTES**   TOTAL **2 HOURS, 30 MINUTES**   SERVES **8**

Do yourself and your guests a favor and find fresh, ripe tomatoes for this recipe that should be made only in summer when tomatoes are in season and at their sweetest. From cherry and grape to Campari and baby San Marzano, bite-size heirlooms come in an array of shapes and sizes and a rainbow of colors that make such a striking presentation.

2 pounds cherry, grape, or other
   bite-size heirloom tomatoes

$2/3$ cup olive oil

$1/3$ cup tarragon vinegar

$1/3$ cup finely chopped fresh flat-leaf
   parsley, plus more for garnish

$1/3$ cup finely chopped fresh chives

1 tablespoon chopped fresh thyme

2 teaspoons minced garlic
   (about 2 garlic cloves)

1 $1/4$ teaspoons table salt

$1/4$ teaspoon black pepper

Fresh thyme leaves (optional)

1 Combine ice and water in a large bowl. Bring a pot of water to a boil. Add the tomatoes to the water, 10 at a time; boil for 30 seconds. Remove the tomatoes with a slotted spoon, and immediately place in the bowl of ice water. Repeat the process until all the tomatoes have been blanched. Peel the tomatoes with the tip of a knife, and place the peeled tomatoes in a large bowl.

2 Whisk together the oil and vinegar in a medium bowl. Stir in the $1/3$ cup parsley, chives, thyme, garlic, salt, and pepper. Pour the dressing over the tomatoes. Cover and chill 2 hours, occasionally spooning the dressing over the tomatoes. Just before serving, place a colander over a bowl, and place the tomato mixture in the colander to drain, reserving the dressing. Transfer the drained tomatoes to a serving dish; garnish with fresh thyme leaves, if desired. Serve with the dressing.

Sidney's Potato Salad

HANDS-ON **40 MINUTES** TOTAL **2 HOURS** SERVES **8**

Whoever Sidney was, when she handed over this recipe for the original Southern Living Party Cookbook *back in 1972, she really wanted to drive home the instruction about not overmixing the potatoes. I think this is the only time I have ever, in all of my years, seen the word "violently" used in a recipe's directions. I have to say, I am with Sidney on this one. Using a violent mixing hand on this potato salad will result in mashed potatoes, which would be a major party foul.*

4 ½ pounds medium-size
   red potatoes (12 potatoes)
½ teaspoon table salt, plus
   more to taste
¾ cup chopped scallions
   (4 scallions)
1 small green bell pepper,
   chopped (¾ cup)

1 cup mayonnaise
½ cup zesty Italian dressing
¾ teaspoon garlic salt
½ teaspoon black pepper,
   plus more to taste
½ teaspoon seasoned salt
   (such as Lawry's)
⅛ teaspoon dried basil

1 Place the potatoes in a large saucepan; sprinkle with ½ teaspoon table salt, and add water to cover the potatoes. Bring to a boil over high. Reduce the heat to medium-high; cover and boil until tender, about 20 minutes. Drain and cool completely, about 1 hour.

2 Slice or cut the potatoes into ¾-inch cubes. Place in a large bowl with the scallions and bell pepper.

3 Combine the mayonnaise, dressing, garlic salt, ½ teaspoon black pepper, seasoned salt, and basil in a separate bowl. Add to the potatoes; toss well, but not violently, to avoid breaking up the potatoes. Season to taste with additional table salt and black pepper, if desired. Serve immediately, or cover and chill until ready to serve.

Note

The secret of this salad is the method of seasoning. By combining the seasoning with the dressing before pouring over the potatoes, the seasoning is more thoroughly incorporated into each piece of the potato.

Chewy Brownie Ice-Cream Sandwiches

HANDS-ON **20 MINUTES**   TOTAL **3 HOURS, 20 MINUTES, INCLUDING FREEZING TIME**   SERVES **12**

These ice-cream sandwiches are a way to end the meal with an exclamation point, not a period. The look of surprise and pure joy on my guests' faces gets me every time. When we are short on time, I purchase mini ice-cream sandwiches and pass them around on silver trays for dessert. That's what I call being smart while making an impression.

¾ cup (6 ounces) salted butter

1 (4-ounce) 60% cacao bittersweet chocolate bar, chopped

1 ¼ cups granulated sugar

2 large eggs

1 cup (about 4 ¼ ounces) all-purpose flour

1 teaspoon vanilla extract

¼ teaspoon baking powder

⅛ teaspoon table salt

Vanilla ice cream, softened

1 Preheat the oven to 350°F. Line the bottom and sides of a 15- x 10-inch jelly-roll pan with aluminum foil, allowing 2 to 3 inches to extend over the sides; lightly grease the foil with cooking spray.

2 Microwave the butter and chocolate in a large microwave-safe bowl at HIGH 1 ½ to 2 minutes or just until melted and smooth, stirring every 30 seconds. Whisk in the sugar. Add the eggs, 1 at a time, whisking just until blended after each addition. Whisk in the flour, vanilla, baking powder, and salt. Pour the mixture into the prepared pan.

3 Bake in the preheated oven for 18 to 20 minutes or until a wooden pick inserted in the center comes out with a few moist crumbs. Cool completely on a wire rack.

4 Lift the brownies from the pan, using the foil as handles. Remove the foil; cut in half crosswise.

5 Spread the softened ice cream onto one brownie half. Top with the remaining brownie half, pressing to allow the ice cream to reach the sides.

6 Wrap with plastic wrap, and freeze 2 hours or until firm. Cut into 12 rectangles and serve immediately, or wrap each sandwich individually with plastic wrap, and freeze until ready to serve.

TAILGATE

Lord, have mercy, I could write about my football memories with my eyes closed. I grew up a Mississippi State University fan and always went to football games with my daddy. It was such a big part of who we were as a family, and some of my best memories from growing up took place in Davis Wade Stadium.

Now fast-forward 25 years and I live smack dab in the middle of Oxford, Mississippi. For those of you who don't follow SEC football, let me bring you up to speed. The University of Mississippi and Mississippi State University couldn't be bigger rivals. Early on, I played the good sport and just bit my tongue, but I have quickly gotten acclimated to The Grove—tailgating Mecca—over the years. I never played sports, but buddy when I get in that Grove it is game on! I know that when we leave our tent to head into the stadium, regardless of how the Rebels play, I won the tailgate. On that, you can bet your life.

For a successful tailgate, you want to be sure to serve on platters that won't break. Melamine, metal, and wood are great choices. You'll thank me for this suggestion when it's time to clean up after the game, in the dark, and with a couple of bourbons under your belt. Always prepare food that is easy to pick up with one hand and eat so you and your guests never have to think about putting your drinks down! Finger sandwiches, sliders, chicken tenders, pickup sweets, and high-fat dips (always the hit of the tailgate even though they don't do anything to help the size of your hiney) are all great ideas. Festive disposables—printed napkins, paper plates in school colors, and cups with your team's logo are a must. Follow these tailgate rules for a big win every game. After all, we may not win every game at Ole Miss, but we never lose a party.

Deviled Eggs

HANDS-ON **15 MINUTES**   TOTAL **30 MINUTES**   SERVES **16**

Deviled eggs have become very trendy. Chefs are topping them with everything from caviar and truffle oil to bacon jam. Use them as a blank canvas and be creative.

16 large eggs

½ cup mayonnaise

2 teaspoons yellow mustard

¼ teaspoon seasoned salt
   (such as Lawry's)

1 teaspoon fresh lemon juice
   (from 1 lemon)

Hot sauce (such as Tabasco)

¼ teaspoon black pepper

Paprika

Chopped fresh flat-leaf parsley

1 Combine ice and water in a large bowl. Place the eggs in a large saucepan; add water to cover. Bring the water to a boil over high, and boil 1 minute. Remove from the heat, cover, and let stand 10 minutes.

2 Drain the eggs, and plunge into the ice water. When cool, remove the shells, and cut the eggs in half lengthwise. Scoop out the yolks into a bowl, reserving the whites. Mash the yolks with a fork. Add the mayonnaise, mustard, seasoned salt, lemon juice, desired amount of hot sauce, and pepper; stir until well combined. Spoon or pipe the yolk mixture into the egg whites. Garnish with the paprika and parsley, if desired.

CAVIAR-AND-SOUR CREAM-TOPPED EGGS: Prepare the recipe as directed, adding 2 teaspoons grated onion to the yolk mixture. Top the filled eggs with a little sour cream and a small amount of red or black caviar.

Herbed Hamburger Sliders

HANDS-ON **30 MINUTES**   TOTAL **40 MINUTES**   SERVES **12**

When grilling hamburgers, place the patties on the hot grate and let them sit. Don't be alarmed — they will immediately stick to the hot grates like white on rice. As soon as they are ready to be flipped they will release from the grate. The biggest mistake you could make is to panic, think they are burning, and scrape the poor patties with a giant spatula. All the crusty goodness is left on the grill, and all you're left with are naked patties.

4 pounds ground chuck	**1 tablespoon kosher salt**
2 large eggs, lightly beaten	**1 teaspoon black pepper**
1 cup finely chopped yellow onion	**¼ teaspoon ground nutmeg**
1 cup herb-flavored stuffing mix	**24 slider buns**
¼ cup Worcestershire sauce	**Lettuce, tomato, cheese, and**
¼ cup chopped fresh flat-leaf parsley	**condiments, for serving**

1 Preheat the grill to medium-high (450°F). Stir together the ground chuck, eggs, onion, stuffing mix, Worcestershire sauce, parsley, salt, pepper, and nutmeg in a large bowl until combined. Shape into 24 (3 ½-inch) patties.

2 Grill, uncovered, until the burgers are cooked through, about 4 minutes per side. Place the burgers on the slider buns, and serve with garnishes and condiments.

Note

A great hamburger begins with the patty.
When forming the patties, it's very important to
not overwork the meat. Mix it as gently as possible,
or your hamburgers will get tough and chewy.

Janie's Baked Beans

(photograph on page 230)

HANDS-ON **15 MINUTES**   TOTAL **2 HOURS, 5 MINUTES**   SERVES **ABOUT 25**

You have to try this original recipe from the 1972 Southern Living Party Cookbook. I have no idea who Janie is, but I wish we could be friends because it seems we have a lot in common. I am sure you are wondering how in the world I know this. It is very simple: We both put sausage in our baked beans. This fact alone says a lot about us. Note that I said "sausage" and not "hot dogs"…do not be one of those people who puts cut up hot dogs (or, God forbid, Vienna sausages) in the baked beans.

2 pounds ground pork sausage

2 cups chopped yellow onion (from 1 large onion)

3 (28-ounce) cans baked beans, undrained

³/₄ cup packed light brown sugar

¹/₂ cup yellow mustard

¹/₄ cup molasses

1 tablespoon dry mustard

1 teaspoon table salt

¹/₂ teaspoon black pepper

1   Preheat the oven to 350°F. Cook the sausage and onion in a large ovenproof Dutch oven over medium-high until the sausage is browned, stirring to crumble. Remove from the heat; drain the sausage mixture in a colander. Return the sausage mixture to the Dutch oven, and stir in the beans, brown sugar, yellow mustard, molasses, dry mustard, salt, and pepper.

2   Cover and bake the beans in the preheated oven for 1 hour. Uncover and cook until thickened, 25 to 30 more minutes, stirring after 10 minutes. Let stand 15 minutes before serving.

Caramelized Onion Dip

(photograph on page 229)

HANDS-ON **1 HOUR**   TOTAL **1 HOUR, 30 MINUTES**   SERVES **16**

This dip is so reminiscent of the French onion dip in a plastic tub that we used to have at sleepover parties when I was growing up. Make sure you gently cook the onions and add a bit of salt, which will help pull out the moisture in the onion and intensify its sweetness.

8 thick-cut bacon slices, chopped

2 tablespoons canola oil

4 large sweet onions, finely chopped (about 8 cups)

2 tablespoons apple cider vinegar

2 (16-ounce) containers sour cream

2 teaspoons kosher salt

1 teaspoon black pepper

5 tablespoons finely chopped chives

Ruffled potato chips

1 Cook the bacon in a large skillet over medium, stirring occasionally, until crisp, about 8 minutes. Transfer with a slotted spoon to a plate lined with paper towels. Reserve 3 to 4 tablespoons of drippings in the skillet.

2 Add the oil to the bacon drippings, and increase the heat to medium-high. Add the onions, and cook, stirring frequently, until softened, about 3 minutes. Reduce the heat to medium-low, and cook, stirring occasionally, until deeply browned and very soft, about 30 minutes. Spoon the onions into a large bowl. Stir in the vinegar. Let stand until cooled to room temperature, about 30 minutes.

3 Add the sour cream, salt, pepper, 1 cup of the bacon, and ¼ cup of the chives to the onions; stir until well combined. Top with the remaining bacon and chives. Serve chilled or at room temperature with the potato chips.

Toffee Bars

HANDS-ON **15 MINUTES**   TOTAL **1 HOUR, 5 MINUTES**   SERVES **24**

Here is another recipe from the original book that is great to have in your arsenal for any sort of get-together. Sometimes when we give parties, I wrap a toffee bar in a clear plastic bag tied with a ribbon. It's a cute way to send guests off with a sweet treat for a bedtime snack.

1 cup (8 ounces) salted butter,
   softened

1 cup packed light brown sugar

1 teaspoon vanilla extract

½ teaspoon maple extract
   (optional)

2 cups (about 8 ½ ounces)
   all-purpose flour

¼ teaspoon table salt

1 cup semisweet chocolate chips

1 cup coarsely chopped toasted
   walnuts or pecans

1   Preheat the oven to 325°F. Beat the butter, brown sugar, vanilla, and, if desired, maple extract in a large bowl with an electric mixer at medium speed until well blended and creamy, about 3 minutes. Add the flour and salt; beat until combined. Stir in the chocolate chips and nuts. Spread into an ungreased 15- x 10-inch baking pan.

2   Bake in the preheated oven until lightly browned, about 20 minutes. While warm, cut into 2- x 1-inch bars. Cool completely in the pan on a wire rack, about 30 minutes.

Tip

When spreading the dough in the pan, be sure that the edges of the dough are slightly thicker than in the center; thin edges tend to brown more quickly than the rest of the dough. Store the bars in an airtight container.

CHUCK WAGON DINNER

- Avocado Dip with Tortilla Chips
- Cowboy Steaks
- Texas-Style Ranchero Beans
- Mrs. R's Coleslaw
- German Potato Salad
- Texas Sheet Cake with Choc Icing

CHUCK WAGON DINNER

Okay Texas and Oklahoma, now I am speaking your language! Many years ago, we drove all the way out to Jackson Hole, Wyoming, from Memphis, Tennessee. My daughter Stott was just two years old. I thought I would lose my religion (more than once) on the way there. My prayer was: Dear Lord, please keep my hands close to the cross and away from Luke's neck.

Luke's daddy, PawPaw, had rented a house and the whole family went to visit. He was nothing more than an overgrown camp counselor with activities planned from morning to night. I must say my favorite was the chuck wagon dinner. We all loaded up into an old-fashioned covered wagon and rode out to the middle of nowhere. When we arrived, there was nothing but stars, mountains, and glowing campfires. It was magical. The meal was prepared in big Dutch ovens and cast-iron skillets over the open fires. The smell of steaks cooking whetted our appetites. It was a no-fuss meal—just simple, straightforward food that was absolutely delicious. Eating in the great outdoors makes everything taste better.

You can re-create this dinner even if you don't live in Texas or Wyoming. If you have a fire pit, you're halfway there. Make sure you have a grate that fits over the fire. Once the fire has burned down to ashen coals and the steaks are seasoned, it's go time. To be extra adorable, wrap colored bandanas around Mason jars to hold utensils, and place them on the buffet next to the plates. Cover bales of hay with quilts to create a comfy, relaxing setting. Galvanized pails and cast iron make fabulous serving pieces for a charming outdoor evening. Once you ring the dinner bell, you can bet that cowboys and cowgirls of all ages will come galloping to fill their plates.

Avocado Dip
with Tortilla Chips

HANDS-ON **10 MINUTES**   TOTAL **1 HOUR, 10 MINUTES**   SERVES **8**

Mayonnaise in an avocado dip? I understand your surprise, but I have to say that it makes this dip pretty fantastic. Covering the avocados with mayonnaise keeps them from turning brown since they aren't exposed to the air, making this a "do the day before" recipe to add to your arsenal. You're welcome!

2 large ripe avocados

¼ cup mayonnaise

1 tablespoon fresh lime juice
   (from 1 lime)

1 canned green chile, minced,
   or ½ teaspoon chili powder

1 small garlic clove, minced

½ teaspoon kosher salt, plus more
   to taste

4 bacon slices, cooked and crumbled

Tortilla chips

Mash the avocados, mayonnaise, and lime juice in a small bowl just until combined. Add the chile, garlic, and ¼ teaspoon salt; stir well. Cover with plastic wrap, placing the plastic wrap directly on the surface of the dip. Chill at least 1 hour. (Dip may be prepared the day before.) Season to taste with salt before serving. Garnish with the crumbled bacon, and serve with tortilla chips.

Cowboy Steaks

HANDS-ON **20 MINUTES**   TOTAL **1 HOUR**   SERVES **6 TO 8**

To ensure that your steak has a beautiful caramelized crust, dry the meat thoroughly before cooking. I have chef friends that take this step so seriously that they use a ShamWow towel to remove excess moisture. The lengths we will go to in order to achieve perfection are amazing!

2 (1 ½- to 2-pound) bone-in rib-eye or
   porterhouse steaks (about 2 inches thick)
Kosher salt and freshly ground black pepper
2 tablespoons vegetable oil

6 tablespoons butter
16 fresh herb sprigs (such as thyme,
   rosemary, and oregano)
6 garlic cloves, peeled and smashed

1 Preheat the grill to medium-high (400° to 450°F). Heat a large cast-iron skillet on the grill, covered with grill lid, 15 minutes. Sprinkle the steaks generously with salt and pepper.

2 Add the oil to the hot skillet. (The oil should smoke.) Using tongs, place the steaks in the skillet, and cook on the grill, uncovered, 10 minutes or until dark brown and crusty. Turn the steaks on the fatty edges in the skillet, holding upright with the tongs, and cook 2 minutes. Place the steak, uncooked sides down, in the skillet. Grill, covered with the grill lid, 8 to 10 minutes or to the desired degree of doneness. (We recommend an internal temperature of 120° to 125°F for medium-rare; the temperature will rise as the steak rests.)

3 Add the butter, herbs, and garlic to 1 side of the skillet, and cook 2 to 3 minutes or until the butter foams. Tilt the skillet slightly, and spoon the butter mixture over the steaks 20 times (being careful not to splatter). Transfer the steaks, herbs, and garlic to a platter; let stand for 5 to 10 minutes. Slice against the grain.

Texas-Style Ranchero Beans

HANDS-ON **25 MINUTES**   TOTAL **11 HOURS, 55 MINUTES,**
INCLUDING 8 HOURS SOAKING TIME   SERVES **8**

These beans are very different from the sweet baked beans that are served at backyard barbecues. The smoky flavor from the cumin is unforgettable and has a distinct Texas taste.

1 pound dried pinto beans

4 ancho chiles, stemmed and seeded

6 cups water

1 tablespoon canola oil

1 ½ cups chopped yellow onion
   (about 1 medium onion)

2 tablespoons minced garlic
   (6 garlic cloves)

1 teaspoon paprika

1 teaspoon ground cumin

½ teaspoon dried oregano

1 (14.5-ounce) can whole peeled
   plum tomatoes, undrained

1 teaspoon light brown sugar

1 teaspoon apple cider vinegar

4 teaspoons kosher salt

¾ teaspoon black pepper

Tortillas or tortilla chips (optional)

1 Place the beans in a large bowl, and cover with 2 inches of water. Let stand at room temperature for 8 hours or overnight. Drain.

2 Heat a large saucepan over medium-high. Add the chiles, and cook, turning occasionally, until the skins start to bubble and pop, about 2 minutes per side. Microwave 2 cups of the water in a microwave-safe glass measuring cup on HIGH until hot, about 2 minutes. Transfer the chiles to a bowl, and cover with the hot water. Let stand until rehydrated and pliable, about 30 minutes.

3 Add the oil to the saucepan, and heat over medium-high until shimmering. Add the onion; cook, stirring frequently, until softened and tender, about 10 minutes. Add the garlic, paprika, cumin, and oregano; cook until the garlic is tender and the spices are toasted, about 1 minute. Transfer the onion mixture to a blender. Add the chiles, tomatoes, brown sugar, and vinegar. Remove the center piece of the blender lid to allow steam to escape. Secure the lid; place a clean towel over the opening in the lid, and process until smooth.

4 Transfer the chile puree to a large Dutch oven. Add the beans, remaining 4 cups water, salt, and pepper; bring to a boil over high. Cover, reduce the heat to medium-low, and cook until slightly tender and creamy, about 2 ½ hours. Uncover, and continue to cook until the liquid thickens to a sauce-like consistency and the beans are tender and creamy, about 30 minutes. Serve hot with tortillas or tortilla chips, if desired.

Mrs. R's Coleslaw

(photograph on page 243)

HANDS-ON **40 MINUTES**   TOTAL **1 HOUR, 40 MINUTES**   SERVES **8**

Feel free to use store-bought mayonnaise for this recipe. If you are feeling guilty about that, take your store-bought mayo and add a little freshly squeezed lemon juice and paprika. Presto! It's sort of like homemade mayo!

1 cup mayonnaise

¼ cup white vinegar

2 tablespoons yellow mustard

1 teaspoon kosher salt

½ teaspoon black pepper

1 head green cabbage (about
   3 pounds), shredded

1 celery stalk, chopped (⅓ cup)

2 green bell peppers, chopped
   (2 ½ cups)

2 red bell peppers, chopped
   (2 ½ cups)

1 medium-size red onion,
   chopped (1 cup)

Whisk together the mayonnaise, vinegar, mustard, salt, and pepper in a large bowl. Add the cabbage, celery, bell peppers, and onion to the dressing; stir until well combined. Chill at least 1 hour, and stir well before serving.

PARTY RULE NO. 9

Better safe than sorry

Let's face it. Heat and humidity are a breeding ground for bacteria. Sure, you want your party to be memorable, but for all the right reasons. Protect your guests from food-borne illnesses by washing hands, cooking foods to optimal temperatures, avoiding cross-contamination, and keeping hot foods hot and cold foods chilled for the duration of the party.

German Potato Salad

(photograph on page 243)

HANDS-ON **15 MINUTES**   TOTAL **35 MINUTES**   SERVES **8**

This salad is best served warm, but it's still a crowd-pleaser at room temperature. It is ideal for any outdoor event because it doesn't include mayonnaise. Long afternoons on the picnic table won't make it any less appetizing or unsafe.

2 pounds red baby new potatoes

8 ounces thick-cut bacon slices, chopped

½ cup finely chopped shallots (about 2 medium shallots)

⅓ cup apple cider vinegar

2 tablespoons granulated sugar

1 tablespoon whole-grain mustard

1 teaspoon kosher salt

1 teaspoon black pepper

¼ cup thinly sliced scallions

2 tablespoons chopped fresh flat-leaf parsley

1 Place the potatoes in a large pot with salted water to cover. Bring to a boil over high. Reduce the heat to medium, and simmer until the potatoes are tender, 10 to 15 minutes. Drain well. Cut the potatoes in half.

2 Cook the bacon in a large skillet over medium, stirring frequently, until crispy, about 10 minutes. Transfer with a slotted spoon to a plate lined with paper towels. Pour the hot drippings over the shallots in a medium bowl. Add the vinegar, sugar, mustard, salt, and pepper, stirring to combine. Toss together the vinaigrette, potatoes, cooked bacon, scallions, and parsley in a large bowl. Serve warm or at room temperature.

Texas Sheet Cake
with Chocolate Icing

HANDS-ON 20 MINUTES   TOTAL 1 HOUR, 30 MINUTES, INCLUDING CHOCOLATE ICING   SERVES 12 TO 15

The saying "everything is bigger and better in Texas" always annoyed me. I am from Mississippi, and I found this notion a little egotistical. That is until I had this cake. After getting halfway through it, I wholeheartedly agreed. Long live Texas!

2 cups granulated sugar

2 cups (about 8 ½ ounces)
   all-purpose flour

½ cup (4 ounces) salted butter

½ cup vegetable shortening

¼ cup (about ⅞ ounce)
   unsweetened cocoa

1 cup water

½ cup whole buttermilk

2 large eggs, lightly beaten

1 teaspoon baking soda

1 teaspoon vanilla extract

Chocolate Icing (recipe follows)

1 Preheat the oven to 400°F. Grease and lightly flour a 15- x 10-inch jelly-roll pan. Sift together the sugar and flour in a large bowl; set aside.

2 Combine the butter, shortening, cocoa, and water in a medium saucepan over medium-high. Bring to a boil, stirring constantly, until melted. Remove from the heat, and pour over the sugar mixture, stirring until dissolved. Cool slightly. Stir in the buttermilk, eggs, baking soda, and vanilla. Pour into the prepared pan.

3 Bake in the preheated oven for 20 minutes. (The cake will have a fudge-like texture.) Immediately spread the warm cake with the Chocolate Icing. Cool completely in the pan (about 1 hour).

Chocolate Icing

½ cup (4 ounces) salted butter

¼ cup (about ⅞ ounce)
   unsweetened cocoa

⅓ cup whole milk

1 (16-ounce) package powdered sugar

1 teaspoon vanilla extract

1 cup chopped pecans

Combine the butter, cocoa, and milk in a medium saucepan. Cook over low 5 minutes or until the butter melts. Bring to a boil over medium. Remove from the heat, and stir in the powdered sugar, vanilla, and pecans. Beat with an electric mixer at medium speed until smooth and the powdered sugar dissolves. **Makes 4 cups**

Southern Living

COOKOUTS
THE SOUTHERN LIVING PARTY COOKBOOK

Lowcountry Boil

LOWCOUNTRY SHRIMP BOIL · COCKTAIL SAUCE
SQUASH PUPPIES · LOWCOUNTRY SIMPLE SLAW
FROZEN PEACHES 'N' CREAM

LOWCOUNTRY BOIL

Not all of us have the luxury of living by the ocean, so you'd think that this Lowcountry Boil would be a party for the lucky few to enjoy. Well, not so fast.

When I was growing up we went to the beach every summer. I looked forward to it all year long. That week always flew by way too fast. One way we extended our beach vacation was by bringing a little bit of the beach back with us. And I don't mean the sand on the floorboard of the car! We went to the local fish market or to the docks to fill up coolers with fresh shrimp. I think this was the only way Daddy got us to leave the beach. He knew if we had something to look forward to at home there would be less whining and tears as we packed up.

On the way home we called our friends and put them on notice that the shrimp boil was on! Before we even unloaded the car, Daddy set up the big pots he used to cook crawfish for boiling the shrimp. Mama would make cocktail sauce, melted butter, and a simple slaw and the party was off and running.

Daddy had us kids gather all the newspapers that had piled up while we were gone and spread them out on the table. Once the shrimp were boiled and drained, Daddy would dump them directly on the newspaper-covered table and all our friends and family would dig in, peeling and eating as fast as we could. You see, while we were enjoying the ocean breezes, our friends and family had been sweating and swatting mosquitos. They couldn't have been any more grateful that we brought a taste of the easy, breezy beach home with us.

Lowcountry Shrimp Boil

HANDS-ON **30 MINUTES**   TOTAL **13 HOURS, INCLUDING SAUCE CHILL TIME**   SERVES **12**

When I work with brides from the East Coast, they think it is a fun idea to suggest including a Lowcountry Boil at their wedding receptions. I quickly explain that this meal needs a few things: a warm sunny day, fresh seafood, and casual clothes. Even bathing suits are acceptable, but they never, ever include high heels, ties, or tuxes. . .and definitely not a white wedding dress.

5 quarts water

¼ cup Old Bay seasoning

4 pounds small red potatoes

2 pounds kielbasa (Polish sausage) or hot smoked sausage, cut into 1 ½-inch pieces

6 ears fresh corn, halved

1 lemon, sliced

4 pounds large unpeeled raw shrimp

Old Bay seasoning

Cocktail Sauce (recipe follows)

Lemon wedges

Hot sauce (such as Tabasco)

1 Bring the 5 quarts water and ¼ cup Old Bay seasoning to a rolling boil in a large covered stockpot.

2 Add the potatoes; return to a boil, and cook, uncovered, 10 minutes. Add the sausage and corn, and return to a boil. Cook 10 minutes or until the potatoes are tender.

3 Add the lemon slices and shrimp to the stockpot; cook 3 to 4 minutes or until the shrimp turn pink. Drain. Serve with Old Bay seasoning, Cocktail Sauce, lemon wedges, and hot sauce.

Cocktail Sauce

2 cups chili sauce (such as Heinz)

½ cup minced celery (about 2 to 3 stalks)

½ cup chopped fresh flat-leaf parsley

⅓ cup Worcestershire sauce

¼ cup prepared horseradish

¼ cup fresh lemon juice (from 2 lemons)

¼ teaspoon kosher salt

⅛ teaspoon hot sauce (such as Tabasco)

⅛ teaspoon granulated sugar

Stir together all the ingredients in a medium bowl. Cover and chill at least 12 hours before serving. Store in the refrigerator up to 1 week. **Makes about 3 ½ cups**

Party Games

As much as adults at any party may relish a laid-back evening, kids (and kids at heart) often have plenty of energy to burn. When a party is outside, it's never a bad idea to have a few outdoor games ready and waiting for kids of all ages. Activities that foster interaction are great icebreakers that give shy guests an opportunity to ease into the action while having something to focus on other than making conversation. Designate a section of the yard for lawn games like horseshoes, croquet, bocce ball, or cornhole for plenty of good old-fashioned fun. Be sure to rope it off so guests don't stumble over croquet wickets or trip over the horseshoe stake after dark.

Lowcountry Simple Slaw

(photograph on page 251)

HANDS-ON **15 MINUTES**   TOTAL **15 MINUTES**   SERVES **12**

Pickled okra is a staple at my house whether it's eaten straight out of the jar or dunked into a Bloody Mary. Adding pickled okra is an unexpected but zesty addition to a basic slaw recipe.

½ cup apple cider vinegar

½ cup canola oil

¼ cup mayonnaise

¼ cup pickled okra juice

2 tablespoons honey

1 teaspoon salt

½ teaspoon black pepper

½ teaspoon celery seeds

2 (16-ounce) packages shredded
    coleslaw mix

2 cups sliced pickled okra

Whisk together the vinegar, canola oil, mayonnaise, pickled okra juice, honey, salt, pepper, and celery seeds in a large bowl. Stir in the coleslaw mix and sliced pickled okra. Serve immediately, or chill up to 24 hours.

PARTY RULE NO. 10

A recipe is a story

Realize that, most times, there's no need to sweat it if you don't have an ingredient called for in a recipe. Just improvise and embellish. No basil? Use parsley instead. Out of pickled okra? Those pickled dilly beans might make the slaw even better. Take a cue from Lowcountry author Pat Conroy, who said, "A recipe is a story that ends with a good meal." Just remember there's more than one way to tell it!

Squash Puppies

HANDS-ON **30 MINUTES**   TOTAL **45 MINUTES**   SERVES **12**

When I was a chef at the Viking Cooking School in Greenwood, Mississippi, we were asked to prepare lunch for the renowned chef Thomas Keller. We were all terrified. What in the world would we cook? We decided not to try anything new and instead stuck with what we knew.

It was the middle of the summer. We all had gardens, which made the menu easy to craft: fried chicken, field peas, butter-poached okra, fried green tomatoes with pimiento cheese, skillet corn, sliced tomatoes with plenty of salt and pepper, homemade mayonnaise, and hush puppies made with my friend Beth's fresh summer squash. Not long after, Thomas Keller said he couldn't remember when he had had a meal as good as the one he had at the cooking school in Greenwood. I wanted to have T-shirts and bumper stickers printed with that quote. On second thought, I just might still do it.

Vegetable oil

¾ cup (about 4 ⅛ ounces)
   self-rising cornmeal mix

¼ cup (about ⅞ ounce)
   all-purpose flour

1 teaspoon table salt

¼ teaspoon black pepper

⅛ teaspoon cayenne pepper

6 medium-size yellow squash,
   cooked and mashed (see Note)

½ cup whole buttermilk

1 small onion, minced

1 large egg

Hot sauce (optional)

Lemon wedges (optional)

1 Pour oil to a depth of ½ inch into a deep cast-iron skillet; heat over medium-high to 350°F.

2 Meanwhile, combine the cornmeal, flour, ½ teaspoon of the salt, black pepper, and cayenne pepper in a large bowl.

3 Stir together the squash, buttermilk, onion, and egg in a separate bowl; add to the cornmeal mixture, stirring just until blended.

4 Scoop the batter by tablespoonfuls, in batches, into the hot oil. Fry 3 minutes on each side or until golden brown. Drain on paper towels; sprinkle evenly with the remaining ½ teaspoon salt. Serve with the hot sauce and lemon wedges, if desired.

Note

6 medium-size zucchini squash may be
substituted for the yellow squash.

Frozen Peaches 'n' Cream

HANDS-ON **15 MINUTES**   TOTAL **8 HOURS, 15 MINUTES,
INCLUDING FREEZING TIME**   SERVES **12**

Peaches are sweet perfection for a fleeting few weeks of summer. Admittedly, it can be a pain to peel two pounds of peaches when you're hot and lazy. The payoff of this recipe is that it preserves that peachy perfection in frozen animation for enjoyment anytime—especially when you're hot and lazy!

**2 pounds ripe peaches, peeled, pitted,
   and quartered (about 10 cups)**

**1 cup granulated sugar, plus more
   to taste**

**1 tablespoon fresh lemon juice
   (from 1 lemon)**

2 cups whipping cream

1 Mash the peaches, including any accumulated juices, with a potato masher. Stir in 1 cup sugar and the lemon juice. Add additional sugar, if necessary.

2 Beat the cream in a separate bowl with an electric mixer at high speed until stiff peaks form. Add to the peach mixture, and stir until well combined. Pour into a 13- x 9-inch freezer-safe dish, and freeze until firm, about 8 hours.

3 Scoop servings with an ice cream scoop into parfait glasses or ice cream cones.

OYSTER ROAST

CUCUMBER-LIME SUMMER BEER
OYSTER ROAST
EASY OYSTER BUTTER
GRILLED ROMAINE WITH CHARRED LEMON-FETA
VINAIGRETTE

OYSTER ROAST

If you live on the coast, you know this is one of the simplest parties to pull together. Oysters have a season just like anything else. Many people say you shouldn't eat oysters in months that don't have an "R" in their name, meaning oysters are their best in September, October, November, December, January, February, March, and April. I really think this stems from when there wasn't proper refrigeration on boats and many people worried that the oysters would spoil if they were harvested during the hot summer months. Regardless of the reason, the rule definitely applies to oyster roasts if only for the dress code.

Sweater weather really should be one of the requirements for a successful oyster roast. After all, the whole party is centered around a hot fire so a little chill in the air works in your favor. Roasting oysters isn't complicated, but it does require a bit of finesse. You need to have a grill that uses charcoal. Once the fire has died down and the coals are ashy, place a very wet (but not dripping or you may extinguish the fire) piece of triple-folded burlap on the grill grate. Spread the oysters over the piece of burlap, and cover the oysters with another piece of wet folded burlap. The steam that the wet burlap creates is crucial for the oysters to roast properly. It should only take about 10 minutes for the oysters to pop open. Once they do, immediately transfer the oysters to the serving table, and serve with seasoned melted butter. To keep the butter melted and piping hot, serve it in galvanized buckets and reheat on the grill as needed.

Besides a salad and some saltine crackers, there really isn't a need to serve anything else. If you have a friend who doesn't like oysters, let them know they will need to bring a sandwich (or be prepared to fill up on saltines)—it's all about the oysters tonight!

Cucumber-Lime Summer Beer

HANDS-ON **5 MINUTES**   TOTAL **1 HOUR, 5 MINUTES,**
INCLUDING CHILLING TIME   SERVES **8**

It's safe to say I drink only three things: water, coffee, and beer. Beer is my friend. I know just how many I can have before becoming tipsy. But make no mistake: This summer beer is not that friend. The rum in it packs a powerful punch. You have been warned.

3 cups prepared limeade (such as Simply Limeade)

¾ cup (6 ounces) white rum

1 cucumber, thinly sliced, plus more for garnish

1 lime, thinly sliced, plus more for garnish

3 (12-ounce) bottles chilled wheat beer (such as Blue Moon)

6 cups crushed ice

1 Combine the limeade, rum, cucumber slices, and lime slices in a large pitcher. Chill about 1 hour.

2 Just before serving, top the limeade mixture with the beer, and stir gently. Divide the ice evenly among 8 glasses; pour the beer mixture over the ice. Garnish with additional cucumber and lime slices, if desired.

Oyster Roast

HANDS-ON **20 MINUTES**   TOTAL **30 MINUTES, INCLUDING BUTTER**   SERVES **8**

When hosting an oyster roast for a larger crowd, make at least 8 to 10 cups of the Easy Oyster Butter recipe. Place it in a clean metal pail and keep it on the grill. This will keep the butter warm and perfect for dousing the oysters in all night long. It's also delicious on steaks, as a topping for green vegetables, or as a spread for French bread.

4 dozen fresh oysters in the shell

Burlap or towel soaked in water

Easy Oyster Butter (recipe follows)

Cocktail Sauce (page 250)

Saltine crackers

Preheat the grill to medium-high (400° to 450°F). Arrange the oysters in a single layer on the grill; cover with wet burlap or towel. Cook, covered with the grill lid, 10 to 12 minutes or until the oysters open. Using tongs, carefully transfer the roasted oysters to a platter. Serve warm with the Easy Oyster Butter, Cocktail Sauce, and saltine crackers.

Easy Oyster Butter

½ cup (4 ounces) unsalted butter, softened

2 teaspoons finely chopped fresh flat-leaf parsley

1 teaspoon finely chopped scallions or chives

1 teaspoon finely chopped fresh dill

1 teaspoon fresh lemon juice (from 1 lemon)

½ teaspoon seasoned salt (such as Lawry's)

½ teaspoon paprika

¼ teaspoon black pepper

Stir together all the ingredients until well blended. Cover and chill until ready to serve.

Makes ½ cup

Grilled Romaine with Charred Lemon-Feta Vinaigrette

HANDS-ON **10 MINUTES**   TOTAL **35 MINUTES**   SERVES **8**

This is a salad that my oldest daughter Stott and I made during the summer before she left for college. After she was gone, I was heartbroken. I couldn't even look at a head of lettuce without bursting into tears. Talk about missing the salad days! Once the romaine is grilled, you'll find that the smoky flavor has penetrated right through the whole head of lettuce. Leave it on the grill a little longer than you think you should; that crispy char only makes it better.

4 romaine lettuce hearts, halved lengthwise

1 lemon, halved crosswise

Cooking spray

6 tablespoons olive oil

2 teaspoons honey

1 teaspoon chopped fresh dill

1 teaspoon kosher salt

½ teaspoon black pepper

3 ounces feta cheese, crumbled (about ½ cup)

1 Preheat a gas grill to high (450° to 500°F) for 15 minutes. Reduce the heat to medium (350° to 400°F).

2 Spray the cut halves of the lettuce and lemon with cooking spray. Place the lettuce and lemon, cut sides down, on the grill grates. Grill, uncovered, until charred, about 30 seconds for the lettuce and 2 to 3 minutes for the lemon. Transfer the lettuce to a platter and the lemons to a cutting board.

3 Squeeze the lemons into a jar with a tight-fitting lid to yield 3 tablespoons juice. Add the oil, honey, dill, salt, and pepper; cover with the lid, and shake until emulsified. Add the feta, and shake once to combine. Drizzle over the lettuce. Serve immediately.

Picnic
ON THE LAWN

Pressed Picnic Sandwich

Farmer's Market Pasta Salad

Ginger and Lime
Marinated Melon Salad

Bertha Mark's Cucumbers

Lemon Drop Cookies

PICNIC ON THE LAWN

MENU FOR 8 TO 10

One of my most favorite people growing up was Marilyn Ragan. She would cut out recipes or articles that she thought I would enjoy and include a comment like, "This would be great for a party." When I moved back to the Delta, I was hired to do all the cooking for Marilyn. You see, Marilyn didn't cook.

Marilyn was a member of many clubs, and you'd think it would be a problem that she didn't cook. It wasn't. She would bring a platter to my house, and I would fix the food. No one was ever the wiser. This was "the" big garden club in town—the one where someone would have to die before they would take a new club member. Every year the club hosted their spring picnic. Each member could invite one guest and was also required to bring a salad. I made six members' salads one year—all on their own platters so they could pass them off as their own. I made sure to arrange different pickup times for the salads so that no one would know that I had made the salads for fellow members.

After all that cooking, I wanted to go out to enjoy lunch somewhere myself. So I called my best friend, Amanda, to see if she would join me. She informed me she was headed out the door as a guest at the spring picnic. When I called my friends Holly, Mary Elizabeth, and Camille, I found out they were headed to the picnic as guests too. So, I gave up, sulked, and ate the leftovers from all the salads I'd spent hours making for half a dozen garden club members.

As soon as the picnic was over, my phone rang and I saw that it was Marilyn. She quickly told me that she'd seen all my friends at the picnic and apologized profusely for not inviting me after I had prepared her salad. Of course I didn't mention I had prepared five other member salads as well, and not a one extended an invitation either. I'll just say, after that, I had a standing invitation to "the" garden club's annual spring picnic—no funeral required.

Pressed Picnic Sandwich

HANDS-ON **30 MINUTES** TOTAL **8 HOURS, 30 MINUTES,**
INCLUDING CHILLING TIME SERVES **10**

Once you build the sandwich, wrap it tightly in plastic wrap. The secret to its success is the pressing part. Personally, I like to use a foil-wrapped brick to weigh down the sandwich in the refrigerator overnight. The crusty baguette will absorb all of the flavorful juices from the layered ingredients to make one amazing sandwich.

2 tablespoons red wine vinegar

1 teaspoon dried oregano

½ teaspoon kosher salt

½ teaspoon black pepper

¼ cup olive oil

1 (12-inch) ciabatta loaf, halved
horizontally, insides scooped out
and discarded

½ cup sun-dried tomato pesto

4 ounces thinly sliced smoked
provolone cheese

8 ounces Genoa salami slices

8 ounces spicy capicola ham slices

1 pound fresh mozzarella cheese,
cut into ¼-inch-thick slices

20 fresh basil leaves

½ cup sliced roasted red peppers

1 Combine the vinegar, oregano, salt, and pepper in a small bowl. Slowly whisk in the oil until emulsified. Brush the vinaigrette over the bottom half of the ciabatta loaf. Spread the pesto over the top half.

2 Layer the provolone slices over the bottom half of the ciabatta, and top with the salami, ham, mozzarella, basil leaves, and red peppers. Cover with the top half of the ciabatta.

3 Wrap the entire sandwich tightly in plastic wrap, and place on a baking sheet or plate. Place a heavy object, such as a skillet, brick, or several books, on top of the sandwich, and chill at least 8 hours or overnight before serving.

4 To serve, unwrap the sandwich, and cut with a serrated knife into 10 slices. It helps to secure each portion with a wooden pick to hold the pressed layers firmly together.

Farmers' Market Pasta Salad

HANDS-ON **20 MINUTES**   TOTAL **30 MINUTES,**
INCLUDING PARMESAN VINAIGRETTE   SERVES **10**

Mason jars are popping up everywhere. People use them for everything from drinks to flower arrangements. They are also the perfect vessel for a layered pasta salad. Add the dressing first so it sits on the bottom and then the salad ingredients. Screw the lid on tight, throw it in a cooler, and head to your favorite picnic spot. Once you arrive, give the jar a good shake and eat it straight out of the jar.

2 cups halved baby heirloom tomatoes

2 small zucchini, thinly sliced into half moons

1 small red bell pepper, cut into thin strips

1 cup fresh corn kernels

1 cup diced firm, ripe fresh peaches
   (about 2 medium)

½ cup thinly sliced scallions

Parmesan Vinaigrette (recipe follows)

1 (8-ounce) package penne pasta
   (see Note)

2 cups shredded smoked chicken
   (about 10 ounces)

⅓ cup torn fresh basil

⅓ cup torn fresh cilantro

1 Toss together the tomatoes, zucchini, bell pepper, corn, peaches, scallions, and vinaigrette in a large bowl, and let stand 10 minutes.

2 Meanwhile, prepare the pasta according to the package directions. Add the hot cooked pasta and chicken to the tomato mixture; toss gently to combine. Season with salt and pepper to taste. Transfer to a serving platter, and top with the basil and cilantro.

Note

1 (20-ounce) package refrigerated
cheese-filled tortellini may be substituted.

Parmesan Vinaigrette

½ cup freshly grated Parmesan cheese

½ cup olive oil

2 teaspoons lemon zest, plus 3 tablespoons
   fresh juice (from 1 lemon)

1 tablespoon balsamic vinegar

2 garlic cloves

2 teaspoons freshly ground black pepper

½ teaspoon table salt

¼ cup chopped fresh basil

¼ cup chopped fresh cilantro

Process the Parmesan cheese, olive oil, lemon zest, lemon juice, balsamic vinegar, garlic, pepper, and salt in a blender or food processor until smooth. Add the basil and cilantro; pulse 5 or 6 times or just until blended. **Makes about 1 cup**

Ginger and Lime Marinated Melon Salad

HANDS-ON **15 MINUTES**   TOTAL **3 HOURS, 15 MINUTES,**
INCLUDING CHILLING TIME   SERVES **8**

This is a far cry from a traditional fruit salad. The cool melon in this salad balances the sharp bite of the grated fresh ginger. I like fruit salad as much as the next person, but there is nothing worse than an underripe melon, mushy strawberries, and seeded grapes. If you cannot find great fruit, please just skip it and move on to a different type of salad.

1 (3 ½-pound) cantaloupe

1 (2-inch) piece fresh ginger, peeled

Cheesecloth or coffee filter

2 tablespoons demerara sugar

1 teaspoon loosely packed lime
   zest, plus 1 tablespoon fresh juice
   (from 1 lime)

¼ teaspoon kosher salt

1 Peel, seed, and slice the cantaloupe into ½-inch-thick wedges. Grate the ginger to equal 1 tablespoon, using the large holes of a box grater. Place the grated ginger in a piece of cheesecloth or a coffee filter. Squeeze the juice from the grated ginger into a large bowl; discard the solids. Add the cantaloupe, sugar, lime zest, lime juice, and salt to the bowl; toss to coat.

2 Pack the mixture into 2 (1-quart) widemouthed canning jars; pour any accumulated juices into the jars. Cover with the metal lids, and screw on the bands. Chill 3 to 8 hours.

Bertha Mark's Cucumbers

HANDS-ON **15 MINUTES**   TOTAL **14 HOURS, 15 MINUTES,
INCLUDING CHILLING TIME**   SERVES **8**

Normally I use high-quality olive oil when I make a vinaigrette, but this is not the time or place for that. This cucumber recipe needs a light oil with a neutral flavor. The vinegar should be the driving flavor and the oil take a back seat.

3 large cucumbers (about 2 ¼ pounds)

2 teaspoons table salt or pickling salt

1 small yellow onion, quartered and
   sliced ¼ inch thick (about 1 cup)

⅔ cup white vinegar

2 tablespoons olive oil

¼ teaspoon black pepper

¼ teaspoon granulated sugar

1 Peel the cucumbers, and cut into ⅛-inch-thick slices. Arrange in layers in a shallow bowl, sprinkling the salt evenly between the layers. Place a plate directly on the cucumbers, and top the plate with a heavy object (such as a can or cast-iron skillet). Let stand at room temperature 2 hours.

2 Drain well, gently pressing the liquid from the cucumbers with the palms of your hands. Place the cucumbers and onions in a 1-quart jar with a tight-fitting lid.

3 Whisk together the vinegar, oil, pepper, and sugar; pour over the cucumbers and onions. Cover with the lid, and chill 12 hours before serving.

Lemon Drop Cookies

HANDS-ON **25 MINUTES**   TOTAL **2 HOURS**   SERVES **24**

You know a lemon dessert hits the mark when you feel a twinge at the back of your jaw. You are sure to get a good pucker with these cookies!

1 ¼ cups (about 5 ⅜ ounces) all-purpose flour

¼ teaspoon baking powder

½ cup (4 ounces) salted butter,
  at room temperature

1 teaspoon lemon zest, plus 2 tablespoons
  fresh juice (from 1 lemon)

¾ cup (3 ounces) powdered sugar

1 tablespoon whole milk

¼ cup crushed lemon-flavored
  hard candies (about 8 candies)

1 Stir together the flour and baking powder in a medium bowl. Set aside. Beat the butter, lemon zest, and ¼ cup of the powdered sugar with a stand mixer at medium speed until creamy, about 2 minutes. Reduce the speed to low, and gradually add the flour mixture, beating until just combined after each addition. Increase the speed to medium, and beat until fully incorporated. Shape the dough into an 8-inch log, and wrap in plastic wrap. Chill at least 1 hour and up to 8 hours.

2 Preheat the oven to 375°F. Slice the dough into ¼-inch-thick rounds. Place about 1 inch apart on a parchment paper-lined baking sheet. Bake in the preheated oven until the bottoms are slightly browned, 10 to 12 minutes. Cool on a baking sheet 2 minutes; transfer the cookies to a wire rack to cool completely, about 20 minutes.

3 Meanwhile, stir together the lemon juice, milk, and remaining ½ cup powdered sugar in a small bowl. Dip the tops of the cookies in the glaze, and sprinkle with the crushed candies. Let stand until set, about 5 minutes.

FISH FRY

Hoppin' John Hushpuppies · Jack's Fried Catfish
Green Tomato Relish · Best Barbecue Slaw
Tartar Sauce Piquant · Sweet Tea Julep Pops

FISH FRY

No matter where you live in the South, guaranteed there's a lake or a river close by, so fish fries are commonplace. It has always been a party that my daddy and his buddies throw. I guess since they catch and clean the fish, it's only right that they fry it on up. Their parties are mainly just a group of men, beers in hand, standing around a vat of hot oil with fish guts scattered everywhere and some paper bags spread on a rickety table. They fry everything—the fish, French fries, hushpuppies, onion rings, and dill pickles. When I was little, I worried they might try to fry me! Although Daddy's gatherings were ten times more fun than any hoity-toity, refined (yes there are fancy ones) fish fry, I can't help but elevate it a bit when I'm hosting my own.

This is such a fun party to throw for a couple's shower. It's a great way to bring two families together in a causal atmosphere with great food. When fried fish is on the menu, the vibe is always laid back. Buckets of beer on ice and a bottle of bourbon never hurt either. Dress the table simply in blue and white, which is a nice contrast to a plate of golden-hued food. A runner made of craft paper lined with condiments, silverware caddies, and low vases of sunflowers or zinnias adds low-cost style.

Now that the stage is set, let the frying begin. An outdoor turkey fryer setup is ideal. This is one of the few times that it's okay to cook while the party is going on. While this goes against my standard rule to prepare most everything for a party ahead of time, I must be flexible for this occasion. After all, cold fried fish is just bad, there's no way around it. Find a friend to be your sidekick at the fryer so you can take turns cooking, and have someone to visit with too. Most of the guests will end up crowded around the fryer anyway, talking and drinking just like my daddy and his buddies used to do.

Hoppin' John Hushpuppies

HANDS-ON **40 MINUTES**   TOTAL **55 MINUTES,**
INCLUDING TOMATO RELISH RECIPE   SERVES **6 TO 8**

If you are ever at a loss when planning a menu, just add a hushpuppy. I honestly can't think of anything they don't work with. Fried chicken. . .Yes! Shrimp boil. . .Yes! Steak. . .Yes! Enchiladas. . .Why not? Ensuring that the oil maintains the right temperature is crucial to making these delicious hushpuppies. The oil should be about 350°F.

Peanut oil

1 (15-ounce) can seasoned field peas
  and snaps, drained and rinsed
  (about 1 cup)

1 cup (about 2 ½ ounces) self-rising
  yellow cornmeal mix

¾ cup whole buttermilk

½ cup (about 2 ⅛ ounces) all-purpose flour

½ cup chopped country ham

½ cup cooked long-grain rice

½ cup sliced scallions, light green
  parts only

1 jalapeño chile, seeded and diced

2 garlic cloves, pressed

1 teaspoon baking powder

1 teaspoon freshly ground black pepper

2 large eggs, lightly beaten

Tomato-Corn Relish (recipe follows)

Hot sauce (optional)

1 Pour the oil to a depth of 3 inches into a large, heavy skillet or Dutch oven; heat over medium-high to 350°F.

2 Meanwhile, stir together the field peas, cornmeal mix, buttermilk, flour, ham, rice, scallions, jalapeño, garlic, baking powder, black pepper, and eggs in a large bowl.

3 Scoop the pea mixture by rounded tablespoonfuls and drop, in batches, into the hot oil. Fry 3 to 4 minutes or until the hushpuppies are golden brown. Drain on paper towels; keep warm. Serve with the Tomato-Corn Relish and hot sauce, if desired.

Tomato-Corn Relish

1 thick bacon slice

1 cup fresh corn kernels (about 1 ear)

1 garlic clove, pressed

1 cup Green Tomato Relish (page 284)

2 teaspoons hot sauce

¼ teaspoon table salt

1 Cook the bacon in a medium skillet over medium-high 3 minutes or until crisp; remove the bacon, and drain on the paper towels, reserving 1 tablespoon drippings in the skillet. Crumble the bacon.

2 Sauté the corn and garlic in the hot drippings 3 minutes or until tender. Stir in the tomato relish, hot sauce, salt, and bacon. Serve immediately. **Makes 1 cup**

Jack's Fried Catfish

HANDS-ON **30 MINUTES** TOTAL **1 HOUR, 40 MINUTES,**
INCLUDING CHILLING TIME AND SAUCE SERVES **6**

Daddy loved to fish with the local commercial fishermen on the Mississippi River. When I was young, he came through the back door full of excitement. My brother and I ran outside to see a catfish as big as we were in the back of his truck. We made the front page of the Bolivar Commercial *newspaper, standing next to the record-breaking catfish. Lordy, we had one hell of a fish fry that night. Good tartar sauce uses lots of lemon juice, and this vintage recipe has lots, as well as lots of unusual ingredients that would make my daddy crazy. Will Gourlay has strong opinions about tartar sauce! Those opinions do not include radishes, olives, or capers. Though he doesn't know what he's missing, let's just keep this recipe between us.*

6 (4- to 6-ounce) catfish fillets

2 cups whole milk

Vegetable oil

2 cups (about 11 ½ ounces) plain
   yellow cornmeal

1 tablespoon seasoned salt
   (such as Lawry's)

2 teaspoons black pepper

½ teaspoon onion powder

½ teaspoon garlic powder

1 teaspoon table salt

1 Arrange the catfish fillets in a single layer in a shallow dish with the milk. Cover and chill 1 hour. Remove from the refrigerator; let stand 10 minutes.

2 Pour 1 ½ inches oil in a large skillet; heat to 350°F. Combine the cornmeal, seasoned salt, pepper, onion powder, and garlic powder in a separate shallow dish.

3 Remove the catfish from the milk; let excess drip off. Sprinkle evenly with the salt. Dredge in the cornmeal mixture, shaking off the excess. Fry, in batches, 3 to 4 minutes per side or until golden. Drain on a wire rack over paper towels.

Tartar Sauce Piquant

1 cup mayonnaise

2 tablespoons fresh lemon juice
   (from 1 lemon)

1 teaspoon minced dill pickles

1 tablespoon minced green olives
   (about 3 olives)

1 tablespoon minced fresh chives

2 teaspoons grated yellow onion

2 teaspoons drained capers

¼ teaspoon hot sauce (such as Tabasco)

⅛ teaspoon black pepper

⅛ teaspoon paprika

3 radishes, peeled and cut into thin
   matchsticks (optional)

Chopped fresh chives and capers

Combine first 11 ingredients in a bowl. Chill at least 1 hour before serving. Garnish with chopped fresh chives and capers before serving. **Makes about 1 ¼ cups**

Green Tomato Relish

HANDS-ON **40 MINUTES**   TOTAL **2 HOURS, 10 MINUTES**   SERVES **8**

One year we had an unusually early frost and had to pick all of the tomatoes when they were still green or lose them altogether. This recipe is one I make to use up my green tomatoes. I love to serve it on a late summer vegetable plate. It really is the icing on the cake.

1 ½ pounds green tomatoes, quartered, seeded, and thinly sliced

1 red bell pepper, thinly sliced

1 poblano chile, thinly sliced

1 large white onion, sliced

1 cup matchstick carrots

½ cup water

2 cups distilled white vinegar (5% acidity)

1 cup granulated sugar

1 tablespoon kosher salt

1 tablespoon mustard seeds

¼ teaspoon ground turmeric

⅛ teaspoon ground cloves

⅛ teaspoon ground allspice

1 Bring the tomatoes, peppers, onion, carrots, ½ cup water, and 1 cup vinegar to a boil in a large stockpot over high; reduce the heat to medium-low, and simmer, stirring occasionally, 30 minutes. Drain.

2 Return the vegetables to the stockpot, and stir in the sugar, salt, mustard seeds, turmeric, cloves, allspice, and remaining 1 cup vinegar. Bring to a boil over medium-high; reduce the heat to medium-low, and simmer 5 minutes. Cool completely. Transfer to a jar; screw on the lid, and chill 30 minutes. Store in the refrigerator up to 1 week.

Best Barbecue Slaw

(photograph on page 282)

HANDS-ON **10 MINUTES**   TOTAL **2 HOURS, 10 MINUTES,**
INCLUDING CHILLING TIME   SERVES **8**

*This recipe is so easy since it uses already shredded cabbage. Make the slaw ahead of time
so you can enjoy your guests and an ice-cold cocktail.*

2 (10-ounce) packages finely
   shredded cabbage

1 carrot, shredded

½ cup granulated sugar

½ teaspoon table salt

⅛ teaspoon black pepper

½ cup mayonnaise

¼ cup whole milk

¼ cup whole buttermilk

2 ½ tablespoons fresh lemon juice
   (from 1 lemon)

1 ½ tablespoons white vinegar

Combine the cabbage and carrot in a large bowl. Whisk together the sugar, salt, pepper,
mayonnaise, milk, buttermilk, lemon juice, and vinegar in a small bowl until blended;
toss with the cabbage mixture. Cover and chill at least 2 hours.

Succulent Centerpiece

Summers in the South often make you feel like you're the fish at a fish fry, but that doesn't mean you can't have a stunning focal point on the patio table all season long. With good drainage and proper planting, succulents thrive in our hot, humid weather. So your table always looks party-ready.

1

FILL A WIDE, SHALLOW DISH three-quarters full with potting mix; cover the top with gravel.

2

BLEND THEM THOROUGHLY, and then moisten with water.

3

REMOVE PLANTS FROM THEIR NURSERY CONTAINERS, and plant the largest one on one side of the pot. Surround it with the other plants, clustering similar shapes together.

4

SPRINKLE DARK-COLORED AQUARIUM GRAVEL around each plant so the soil is covered.

Sweet Tea Julep Pops

HANDS-ON **15 MINUTES**   TOTAL **8 HOURS, 25 MINUTES,**
INCLUDING FREEZING TIME   SERVES **12**

Sweet tea is the house wine of the South, and mint juleps are the signature cocktail. When you combine the two and freeze them into an adult ice pop, it makes for the most delicious Southern treat on earth.

2 cups water

2 family-size tea bags

1 cup firmly packed mint leaves

1 cup cold water

¾ cup bourbon

½ cup granulated sugar

3 tablespoons fresh lemon juice
  (from 1 lemon)

12 (3-ounce) paper cups

12 mint leaves (optional)

12 small lemon slices (optional)

12 (3 ½-inch) wooden ice cream spoons

1 Bring 2 cups water to a boil in a 2-quart saucepan. Remove from the heat, add the tea bags, and stir in 1 cup firmly packed fresh mint leaves. Cover and steep 10 minutes. Discard the tea bags and mint.

2 Stir in 1 cup cold water, the bourbon, sugar, and lemon juice, stirring until the sugar dissolves. Pour the mixture into the paper cups; add a mint leaf and small lemon slice to each, if desired.

3 Cover each cup with aluminum foil; make a small slit in the centers, and insert 1 ice cream spoon into each cup. Freeze 8 hours or until firm.

Celebrations and Dinners

Every party is a celebration, but the ones centered around life's everyday rites of passage and important occasions should always be memorable. There is just something so special about gathering together to note a milestone or raising a glass to honor a goal achieved. The major catch with these sorts of parties is the way every aspect should be thoughtful. Whether you are entertaining a crowd or only a few special guests, you should really put on the dog and pull out all the stops. Go ahead and splurge on that fancy beef tenderloin and those hybrid tea roses. Take time on those beautiful place cards with hand-lettered calligraphy. All those minute details add up to one unforgettable evening.

MARINATED WHOLE BEEF TENDERLOIN

IMPRESS

BÉARNAISE SAUCE

THE

GREEN BEAN-GOAT CHEESE GRATIN

BOSS

SMASHED BABY RED POTATOES

DINNER

ICE CREAM BOMBE

IMPRESS THE BOSS DINNER

MENU FOR 8

I use the term "boss" loosely. Certainly, this dinner will impress the person you work for, but there are lots of people to impress in your life. Maybe it's your mother-in-law or a new fancy friend. Maybe it's the president of a club you are dying to get into or a client you're desperate to land.

One of my most memorable "put on the dog" dinners was for Andy Lack, the president of NBC. I had been asked to cater a 12-person seated dinner at Rowan Oak, William Faulkner's historic home. It was scheduled for a Thursday, and Mr. Lack was resuming his position as head of NBC the following Monday. Why was I so intent on impressing Andy? Well, you see, I'd wanted to be on the TODAY show for 17 years. I figured this was my shot. My amazing right-hand gal and event coordinator, Sarah Virden, had her mother, Martha, drive up from Columbus toting every piece of sterling silver she owned. Martha packed her car from floorboard to ceiling with her collection of gorgeous china and exquisite crystal too.

The night kicked off with mint juleps in sterling silver cups accented with sterling silver straws for sipping. . .and it only got more impressive from there. At the end of the meal and stuffed with good food, Andy grabbed my hands in his and exclaimed that he thought I was wildly talented. With a few bats of my eyelashes and a sassy hair flip I said, "Oh, Andy, I'm sure you tell all the girls that!" He quickly responded, "No I don't, and I have eaten everywhere and everything on earth. You, my dear, are talented." Taking advantage of the moment, I quickly informed him that I was so glad he felt that way because I had always wanted to be on the TODAY show. You know what? I got a call asking me to appear on the show soon after. So far, my good luck has continued. You just never know what might come from impressing the boss. . .or anyone for that matter.

Marinated Whole Beef Tenderloin

HANDS-ON **40 MINUTES**   TOTAL **9 HOURS, 30 MINUTES,**
INCLUDING MARINATING TIME AND SAUCE   SERVES **10**

*A beef tenderloin on the table is the epitome of pulling out all the stops. It's an extremely
expensive cut, but worth every penny. As one of my favorite friends loves to say to his wife,
"Why spend less when you can spend more?" Follow all of these steps to the letter, and you
will have a dynamite dinner on your hands.*

1 (6-pound) whole beef tenderloin,
   trimmed
8 garlic cloves, minced
¼ cup soy sauce
¼ cup dry sherry

¼ cup packed dark brown sugar
1 teaspoon kosher salt
½ teaspoon black pepper
Rosemary sprigs
Béarnaise Sauce (recipe follows)

1 Place the beef, garlic, soy sauce, sherry, and brown sugar in a 2-gallon ziplock plastic
freezer bag. Seal and shake to distribute the marinade and coat the beef. Refrigerate
at least 8 hours or up to 24 hours, turning the bag halfway through.

2 Preheat the oven to 400°F. Remove the beef from the marinade, discarding the
marinade, and pat dry thoroughly. Sprinkle the beef evenly with the salt and pepper.
Place on a rack in a large rimmed baking sheet or roasting pan. Roast in the preheated
oven until a meat thermometer inserted in the thickest portion registers 120°F for
medium-rare, about 55 minutes. (Temperature will rise to 135°F as it stands.) Let the
meat rest, lightly tented with foil, 10 minutes before slicing. Serve warm, garnished
with fresh rosemary, with the Béarnaise Sauce on the side.

Béarnaise Sauce

*Gild that lily. Stir lump crabmeat or bits of steamed lobster into the sauce. You'll have the most
decadent sauce paired with the most decadent seafood for an absolutely winning combination.*

2 tablespoons chopped shallots
   (from 1 small shallot)
2 tablespoons dry white wine
1 tablespoon tarragon vinegar

2 teaspoons chopped fresh tarragon
¼ teaspoon black pepper
Blender Hollandaise Sauce (page 186)

Combine the shallots, wine, vinegar, tarragon, and pepper in a small saucepan. Cook over
medium until almost all the liquid has evaporated, about 2 minutes. Transfer to a blender.
Add the Blender Hollandaise Sauce; cover and process on high 4 seconds. **Makes 1 cup**

Green Bean-Goat Cheese Gratin

(photograph on page 295)

HANDS-ON **20 MINUTES**   TOTAL **53 MINUTES**   SERVES **8**

Using ramekins to serve this recipe makes an elegant impression and presentation. If you want to serve this on a buffet, feel free to skip the ramekins and substitute a 13- x 9-inch baking dish and increase the baking time by 10 minutes.

4 white bread slices

2 tablespoons olive oil

6 ounces Parmesan cheese, shredded
   (1 ½ cups)

⅔ cup finely chopped pecans

2 pounds haricots verts (French
   green beans), trimmed

4 ounces goat cheese, crumbled
   (about 1 cup)

1 cup whipping cream

½ teaspoon kosher salt

½ teaspoon black pepper

1 Preheat the oven to 400°F. Tear the bread into large pieces; pulse in a food processor 2 or 3 times or until coarse crumbs form. Drizzle the oil over the crumbs; add ½ cup of the Parmesan cheese. Pulse 5 or 6 times or until coated with oil. Stir in the pecans.

2 Combine ice and water in a large bowl. Cut the green beans crosswise into thirds. Cook in boiling water to cover 3 to 4 minutes or until crisp-tender; drain. Plunge the beans into the ice water to stop the cooking process; drain and pat dry with paper towels.

3 Toss together the beans, goat cheese, whipping cream, salt, pepper, and the remaining 1 cup Parmesan cheese. Firmly pack the mixture into 8 (6-ounce) shallow ramekins. Cover each with aluminum foil, and place on a baking sheet.

4 Bake in the preheated oven for 20 minutes. Uncover and sprinkle with the crumb mixture. Bake 8 more minutes or until golden brown. Let stand 5 minutes.

Smashed Baby Red Potatoes

(photograph on page 295)

HANDS-ON **10 MINUTES**   TOTAL **45 MINUTES**   SERVES **8**

When I first tried this recipe, I thought to myself, "Why can't we just boil the potatoes, smash them in a bowl, pour the butter mixture over the top, and call it a day?" Then, I tried the recipe and this unusual cooking method results in a spectacular spud. Trust me, don't take the shortcut.

2 pounds red baby new potatoes

4 rosemary sprigs

3 garlic cloves, smashed

¼ cup plus ½ teaspoon kosher salt

¼ cup extra-virgin olive oil

2 tablespoons (1 ounce) unsalted
  butter, melted

1 tablespoon chopped fresh flat-leaf
  parsley

2 teaspoons chopped fresh thyme

1 teaspoon chopped fresh rosemary

1 garlic clove, minced

¼ teaspoon black pepper

1 Preheat the oven to 425°F. Place the potatoes, rosemary sprigs, smashed garlic, ¼ cup of the salt, and water to cover in a 3-quart saucepan. Bring to a boil over high; reduce the heat to medium, and simmer until the potatoes are tender when pierced with a fork, 10 to 15 minutes. Drain; discard the rosemary sprigs and smashed garlic.

2 Brush a rimmed baking sheet with 2 tablespoons of the oil. Arrange the potatoes on the prepared baking sheet. Using the heel of your hand, lightly crush the potatoes until they are about ½ inch thick. Brush with 1 tablespoon of the oil. Bake in the preheated oven until golden brown and crisp, 25 minutes.

3 Stir together the butter, chopped parsley, thyme, rosemary, minced garlic, pepper, and remaining 1 tablespoon oil and ½ teaspoon salt. Brush the mixture over the potatoes, and serve immediately.

Ice Cream Bombe

HANDS-ON **20 MINUTES**   TOTAL **3 HOURS, 50 MINUTES**   SERVES **12**

I know this recipe might look daunting, but I'm here to tell you it's worth it. I am not one to look on the negative side of anything so I will focus on the positives of this recipe. It can be made weeks in advance. It involves not one, not two, but three different types of ice cream. Lastly, no one will ever, I mean ever, forget this dessert.

4 cups vanilla ice cream, softened

2 cups chocolate ice cream, softened

2 cups raspberry sorbet

1 cup fresh raspberries

1 cup fresh blueberries

Mint leaves (optional)

1 Line a large freezer-safe bowl, melon mold, or 13-cup Bundt cake pan with plastic wrap. Spread the vanilla ice cream about 1 inch thick in the mold. Freeze until firm, about 15 minutes. Spread a layer of the chocolate ice cream about 1 inch thick over the vanilla ice cream. Freeze until firm, about 15 minutes. Spread the raspberry sorbet over the chocolate ice cream. Freeze until firm, about 3 hours.

2 To unmold, dip the mold quickly into warm water, then invert onto a serving platter. Garnish with the berries and mint, if desired, and serve immediately.

INFINITE VARIATIONS! Any combination of ice cream may be used: coffee, chocolate, and buttered almond; strawberry, raspberry, and vanilla; or vanilla, and orange or pineapple sherbet. The outer layer should be ice cream rather than sherbet; it holds up better. During the summer, I pile slices of luscious peaches around the base of the mold—or if you're wallowing in luxury, jarred whole marrons (chestnuts) soaked in brandy may be used.

Heather

Bill

Lily

James

Sandy

Fall Dinner

Crabmeat Maryland

Arugula with Warm
Bacon Vinaigrette

American-Style Beef
Bourguignon

Potatoes Dauphinoise

Chocolate Cheesecake

FALL DINNER

One of the happiest days of the year for me is the day the pumpkins arrive at the farmers' market. I love it so much that it is borderline crazy. I end up buying pumpkins every day for a solid month because I always find one more interesting or perfect than the last. From Halloween through Thanksgiving, I use them on the porch, dining table, hollowed out for cut flowers, planted with succulents, or to hold flickering candles. After Thanksgiving, I spray paint them and use them right through the holidays in my Christmas decorations.

If pumpkins get me going, you can imagine how excited I get about hosting the fall supper of the season. This is a meal that I always serve family-style. I set up farm tables outdoors that I decorate with tangles of bittersweet, baby pumpkins, and gourds nestled among the vines. It's also a great time to pull in collected deer antlers, fall leaves, or feathers. I drape mismatched wool blankets on the backs of chairs since the days are getting shorter and evenings are often crisp.

As guests arrive, I greet them with a Honeycrisp apple cocktail made from apple cider and ginger beer spiked with bourbon and served with a honey stick straw. Once guests are seated, I bring out rustic dishes filled with cool-season favorites like peppery arugula salad with a warm vinaigrette dotted with bits of crisp bacon, hot yeast rolls, and a comforting potato gratin. The Beef Bourguignon recipe in this menu is perfect for any family-style meal. It is hearty, rich, and holds its heat beautifully in a big Dutch oven. This is one of those laid-back, pleasant meals that seems to go on forever and that you never want to end.

Once everyone is finished eating, we wrap ourselves in the blankets and have one final drink and laugh around the bonfire. Everyone leaves with an appreciation that autumn is short and truly worth celebrating.

Crabmeat Maryland

HANDS-ON **25 MINUTES**   TOTAL **25 MINUTES**   SERVES **8**

Crabmeat is so luxurious and delicate that the last thing anyone should do is mask its flavor. This recipe approaches it just right. Sherry and cream are the perfect complementary partners for the shellfish. They add depth of flavor without stealing the show.

6 tablespoons (3 ounces) salted
  butter

3 tablespoons all-purpose flour

2 cups whole milk

1 pound fresh lump crabmeat,
  drained and picked over

½ cup heavy cream

½ teaspoon kosher salt

⅛ teaspoon black pepper

¼ teaspoon paprika

2 tablespoons dry sherry

1 tablespoon fresh lemon juice
  (from 1 lemon)

Chopped fresh chives or flat-leaf
  parsley (optional)

Toast points or Melba rounds

1 Melt 4 tablespoons of the butter in a medium saucepan over medium. Add the flour, and cook, whisking constantly, 1 minute. Gradually whisk in the milk, and cook, whisking constantly, until thick and smooth, about 12 minutes.

2 Add the crabmeat, stirring gently to avoid breaking the lumps; cook until heated through, about 1 minute. Gently stir in the cream and remaining 2 tablespoons butter until melted. Stir in the salt, pepper, and paprika. Add the sherry and lemon juice. Cover and keep warm over low until ready to serve.

3 Just before serving, spoon into a chafing dish. Top with the chives or parsley, if desired. Serve over the toast points or with the Melba rounds for dipping.

Arugula with Warm Bacon Vinaigrette

HANDS-ON **10 MINUTES**   TOTAL **10 MINUTES**   SERVES **4**

Warm bacon dressing and spinach salad was the calling card of the 1980s. This arugula salad has all the goodness of that original but with a peppery freshness that keeps it from being boring. It's also amazing with blue cheese, ripe pears, and caramelized onions.

4 bacon slices

1 shallot, minced

¼ cup extra-virgin olive oil

2 tablespoons red wine vinegar

¼ teaspoon kosher salt

¼ teaspoon cracked black pepper

1 (5-ounce) package arugula or
   mixed greens

1½ ounces goat cheese, crumbled
   (about ⅓ cup)

1 Cook the bacon in a large skillet over medium 6 minutes or until crisp. Remove the bacon, reserving the drippings in the skillet. Crumble the bacon. Sauté the shallot in the drippings 2 minutes or just until tender.

2 Transfer the shallot and drippings to a small bowl. Whisk in the oil, vinegar, salt, and pepper. Toss the arugula with the vinaigrette on a serving platter. Top with the goat cheese and bacon.

PARTY RULE NO. 11

Dress for the party

. . . and we're not talking about dressing the lettuce leaves. Creating a festive tone goes beyond setting the table or lighting candles. All the party panache in the world doesn't grant you a sloppy-outfit pass. You may be stressed and tired, but yoga pants and a sweat-wicking tank do not a hostess outfit make. Leave a lasting impression, but be sure it's a good one. There's nothing wrong with casual attire as long as it's clean, neat, and fits the occasion.

American-Style Beef Bourguignon

(photograph on page 308)

HANDS-ON **1 HOUR, 15 MINUTES**   TOTAL **3 HOURS, 45 MINUTES**   SERVES **6**

This French classic was made famous in the U.S. by the one and only Julia Child. The dish is very rich and satisfying, but still elegant enough to impress even your most sophisticated friends. Use good-quality wine you'd want to drink for the best results.

CELEBRATIONS AND DINNERS

306

PARTY COOKBOOK

- 4 bacon slices, cut into ½-inch pieces
- 2 tablespoons olive oil
- 3 pounds boneless chuck roast (or other lean beef), cut in 1-inch cubes
- 2 ½ cups dry red wine
- 1 (10 ½-ounce) can beef consommé
- 1 tablespoon tomato paste
- 1 teaspoon chopped fresh thyme (about 1 sprig)
- 1 teaspoon table salt, plus more to taste
- ½ teaspoon black pepper, plus more to taste
- 1 bay leaf
- 2 large garlic cloves, minced (2 ½ teaspoons)
- 2 ½ cups beef broth, plus more if needed
- 12 pearl onions (9 ounces)
- 3 tablespoons (1 ½ ounces) salted butter
- 1 (8-ounce) package fresh mushrooms, coarsely chopped
- 1 tablespoon all-purpose flour
- Chopped fresh flat-leaf parsley

1 Preheat the oven to 300°F. Cook the bacon in a heavy ovenproof Dutch oven over medium until crisp, about 8 minutes. Transfer with a slotted spoon to a plate lined with paper towels. Reserve 1 tablespoon drippings in the Dutch oven.

2 Add 1 tablespoon of the oil to the drippings; heat over medium-high until hot. Add the beef in 2 batches; cook until well browned, about 2 minutes on each side, adding the remaining 1 tablespoon of oil when adding the second batch of meat. Add ½ cup of the wine to the Dutch oven, and cook, stirring to loosen the browned bits from the bottom of the Dutch oven.

3 Return the bacon and beef to the Dutch oven. Add the beef consommé, tomato paste, thyme, 1 teaspoon salt, pepper, bay leaf, and garlic. Pour in the remaining 2 cups wine or enough to almost cover the meat. Bring just to a boil over medium-high heat. Remove from the heat.

1972 SOUTHERN LIVING PARTY COOKBOOK ORIGINAL

4. Bake, uncovered, in the preheated oven until the meat is tender, stirring occasionally, about 2 ½ hours. As the liquid cooks down, add 1 cup of the beef broth, or more if needed.

5. Meanwhile, prepare the vegetables. Peel the onions and cut a small "x" in the stem ends to prevent them from coming apart during cooking. Place the onions and the remaining 1 ½ cups of the beef broth in a small saucepan. Bring to a boil over medium-high; reduce the heat to low, and simmer until tender, about 20 minutes. Drain the onions, reserving ¾ cup cooking liquid; set aside.

6. Melt 2 tablespoons of the butter in a medium skillet over medium-high. Add the mushrooms, and cook, stirring once or twice, until browned and tender, about 5 minutes. Remove from the heat; set aside.

7. When the beef is done, remove the beef from the braising liquid with a slotted spoon, and place in a large bowl. Add the cooked onions and mushrooms to the bowl.

8. Add the reserved ¾ cup liquid from the cooked onions to the beef braising liquid in the Dutch oven. Skim the fat from the surface of the liquid as needed. Place the Dutch oven over medium-high; bring to a boil.

9. Melt the remaining 1 tablespoon butter in a small saucepan, and stir in the flour until smooth. Gradually stir a small amount (about ¼ cup) of the hot cooking liquid into the flour mixture, then stir the flour mixture into the cooking liquid in the Dutch oven. Add salt and pepper to taste. Add the beef mixture to the Dutch oven; cook over medium until heated through, about 5 minutes. Remove and discard the bay leaf. Serve sprinkled with the parsley.

Notes

Double this recipe to serve 12. But do
not try to cook it all in one Dutch oven.

If fresh pearl onions are not available,
use frozen; thaw them well, and sauté
1 to 2 minutes in butter.

Potatoes Dauphinoise

HANDS-ON **20 MINUTES**   TOTAL **1 HOUR**   SERVES **8**

Deliciously rich, this potato casserole is cheesy goodness. It's a dish you may find yourself eating straight out of the pan at midnight while standing in the glow of the fridge. Of course, I have never done it, but I have heard stories about people who have.

6 medium-size russet potatoes (2 ½ pounds)

3 cups whole milk

½ cup (4 ounces) salted butter, plus more for baking dish

1 teaspoon kosher salt

⅛ teaspoon ground white pepper

2 garlic cloves, minced

4 ounces Swiss cheese, shredded (about 1 cup)

1 Preheat the oven to 350°F. Scrub and peel the potatoes, and then cut them into ⅛-inch-thick slices.

2 Combine the potatoes, milk, butter, salt, and white pepper in a large saucepan. Bring to a simmer over medium. Add the garlic; partially cover the pan and simmer until the potatoes are almost tender when tested with the point of a small sharp knife, about 20 minutes.

3 Pour the potatoes and the liquid into a buttered 13- x 9-inch (3-quart) baking dish. Sprinkle with the cheese. Bake in the preheated oven until the sauce has thickened and the cheese has melted and is golden brown, about 35 minutes.

Note

This dish may be prepared up to the baking point the day before. Sometimes the casserole bubbles over onto the oven floor, creating quite a smoky mess. To avoid this, place a large shallow pan of water or sheet of foil on the lower rack of the oven during cooking.

Chocolate Cheesecake

HANDS-ON **25 MINUTES**   TOTAL **8 HOURS, 35 MINUTES**   SERVES **12**

This crust is made using a very thin chocolate wafer cookie found in most grocery stores. If you prefer, substitute cream-filled chocolate cookies. This cheesecake freezes beautifully—two of the sweetest words to a cook's ears.

CRUST

1 (9-ounce) package thin chocolate
  wafer cookies

⅓ cup (2 ⅔ ounces) salted butter,
  melted

¼ teaspoon ground cinnamon

FILLING

1 (12-ounce) package semisweet
  chocolate chips (2 cups)

4 (8-ounce) packages cream
  cheese, softened

2 cups granulated sugar

4 large eggs

1 tablespoon unsweetened cocoa

2 teaspoons vanilla extract

2 cups sour cream

GANACHE

1 cup semisweet chocolate chips

½ cup whipping cream

Whipped cream (optional)

Shaved chocolate (optional)

1 Prepare the Crust: Preheat the oven to 325°F. Place the chocolate wafer cookies in a food processor; process to fine crumbs, about 20 seconds. Combine the crumbs with the butter and cinnamon; press into the bottom and 1 ½ inches up the sides of a 10-inch springform pan. Bake in the preheated oven until set, about 10 minutes. Remove from the oven, and cool completely on a wire rack, about 30 minutes.

2 Prepare the Filling: Microwave the chocolate chips in a microwave-safe bowl on HIGH 1 minute; stir. Microwave at 30-second intervals until melted. Stir until smooth; set aside. Beat the cream cheese with a stand mixer at medium speed until smooth. Gradually add the sugar until blended. Add the eggs, 1 at a time, beating at low speed until blended after each addition. Add the melted chocolate, cocoa, and vanilla; beat at low speed until blended. Stir in the sour cream. Pour into the prepared crust.

3 Bake in the preheated oven until almost set, 1 hour and 10 minutes. (The center of the cheesecake will jiggle slightly but become firm as it chills.) Remove from the oven; run a knife around the edge of the cheesecake to loosen from the sides of the pan. Cool completely in the pan, about 2 hours. Remove the sides of the pan.

4 Prepare the Ganache: Combine the chocolate chips and cream in a microwave-safe bowl. Microwave on HIGH 1 minute; let stand 30 seconds. Stir until smooth. Pour over the cooled cheesecake. Cover; chill at least 5 hours before serving. Top with the whipped cream and shaved chocolate, if desired.

THANKSGIVING
DINNER

Old-Fashioned Roasted Turkey · Cornbread Dressing
Minnie's Sweet Potato Pone · Simple Pecan-Green Bean Casserole
Cranberry Salad · Chocolate-Bourbon Pecan Pie

THANKSGIVING DINNER

Strap on your stretchy pants, the Super Bowl of all holiday celebrations has finally arrived. I love Thanksgiving because it focuses on gratitude and food: two of my favorite things.

This is the one holiday that for years I let anyone bring anything that they wanted to add to the mix of dishes. One year, Luke and I hosted Thanksgiving at our cabin at the Merigold Hunting Club. We invited Luke's sister and brother-in-law and our nephew. I planned the menu weeks in advance. I would serve my grandmother's and mother's recipes that have been on the table every Thanksgiving for as long as I can remember—pillowcase-roasted turkey, cranberry sauce, cornbread dressing, sweet potato casserole with mini marshmallows, asparagus with hollandaise, rice with turkey gravy, rolls, and bourbon pecan pie. My sweet sister-in-law Margaret offered to bring something since she had been raised right and knew not to arrive empty-handed. I shared the menu with her and she offered to bring the dressing. I replied that that would be lovely.

For you to understand the horrors of what I am about to tell you, one must understand that cornbread dressing is sacred to me. I love it so much that I eat it only twice a year. I don't ever want it to become a commonplace dish. I also want to defend myself by saying that I had only had my mother's and grandmother's cornbread dressing. I didn't even know there was any other kind of dressing. When Margaret arrived on Thanksgiving morning, she had a grocery bag from Kroger. Inside, there were two boxes of boxed stuffing mix. I kid you not! My blood pressure is rising just remembering it. That was the day I learned that if someone asks if they can bring something to Thanksgiving, quickly reply, "wine!"

Old-Fashioned Roasted Turkey

HANDS-ON **30 MINUTES**   TOTAL **4 HOURS, 45 MINUTES**   SERVES **16**

There is no reason to get all bent out of shape about cooking a turkey. It is nothing more than a big chicken. That's it. Just think 'big chicken' and all that anxiety melts away. If you are still nervous enlist the help of a family member. My brother-in-law Randy has always been my holiday helper. He is my support system, my rock. He makes me laugh just as I am about to have a full-on come-apart. Find your Randy and I can assure you you will sail through the holidays. See the carving instructions beginning on page 316.

1 (14- to 16-pound) whole fresh
  or frozen turkey, thawed
5 tablespoons (2 ½ ounces)
  unsalted butter, melted
1 tablespoon table salt
2 teaspoons seasoned salt
1 teaspoon poultry seasoning

1 teaspoon garlic powder
1 teaspoon paprika
½ teaspoon ground ginger
½ teaspoon black pepper
¼ teaspoon cayenne pepper
¼ teaspoon dried basil
1 cup water

1 Preheat the oven to 350°F. Remove the giblets and neck from the turkey; reserve them for another use. Pat the turkey dry, and remove excess skin. Brush the turkey with 3 tablespoons of the melted butter. Stir together the table salt, seasoned salt, poultry seasoning, garlic powder, paprika, ground ginger, black pepper, cayenne pepper, and dried basil, and rub thoroughly in inside and on outside of bird. Tie the ends of the legs together with kitchen twine, and tuck the wing tips under. Place the turkey, breast side up, on a rack in a roasting pan. Add 1 cup water to the pan, and cover with aluminum foil.

2 Bake in the preheated oven on the lowest rack for 3 hours and 45 minutes. Uncover, and brush the turkey with the remaining 2 tablespoons melted butter. Continue roasting, uncovered, until a thermometer inserted in the thickest portion of the thigh registers 170°F and the skin is browned, about 15 minutes. (If the turkey is overbrowning, reduce the temperature to 300°F for the last half hour of roasting.) Remove from the oven. Cover with aluminum foil, and let rest 15 minutes before slicing and serving.

Carving

Pity the guest who watches a turkey leg wrenched in desperation, a standing rib trip across a platter and gravy dribble on the tablecloth. Carving, an easily learned skill, adds much to the success of a well served meal. Properly carved servings appeal to the eye and the economy—a well carved roast or chicken gives more mileage to the servings.

After removing meat or fowl from the oven, allow it to "set" a few minutes to make the carving easier. Place the meat on a hot platter that is large enough to accommodate the roast or turkey and the portions as they are cut. Garnishes are attractive but should not hamper the carver. Plates should also be warmed to keep food from cooling too quickly.

Carving may be done in the kitchen, the meat or fowl arranged on the hot platter and served piping hot. At the table, the carver may stand or sit, whichever is most comfortable.

The carving knife and fork are placed at the right side. After carving they may be laid together on the platter or one placed at each end of the platter. The importance being that they not drip on the tablecloth.

After the first incision has been made the angle of the knife should not alter. Each cut should be direct, sharp, and incisive made with a long sweeping stroke to give a smooth, even slice. A swaying motion gives a jagged, torn slice.

Cut across the grain of any meat to seal juices and give a tender slice. Steak is the exception but do slice steak at an angle to seal juices.

STANDING RIB ROAST

1. Rib standing, place the heavy end to the carver's left.

2. Insert fork and with knife slice through crispy fat to bone.

3. Cut as many slices as desired before removing fork.

4. Draw knife along bone to separate slices. If the roast is small, one or two ribs, and won't stand, place it on its side with the ribs to the carver. Cut horizontal slices and loosen from the bone with a vertical slice.

ROAST TURKEY OR CHICKEN

1. Place bird breast-side up with legs to carver's right. Remove strings and skewers.

2. Beginning with the side nearest the carver, insert the fork one prong through the drumstick, the other through the second joint (thigh).

3. Use the carving knife to cut around the second joint.

4. With the flat blade, press against the body of the bird and using the fork as a lever, draw the leg toward you. If necessary use the knife to cut through the flesh and skin from the underside of the leg.

5. Place drumstick and second joint on a side platter skin-side down so the joint may be clearly seen and more easily divided.

6. Cut the joint in lengthwise pieces and holding the drumstick heavy-end down, slice for serving.

7. Remove the wing at the joint in much the same manner.

8. Plunge the fork deeply across the breast bone and beginning at the left, carve long even slices of white meat from the breast. Under the back, attached at either side of the back bone, are found two choice bites of dark meat, known as the "oyster."

9. To carve the other side, turn the platter and repeat.

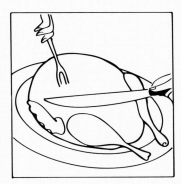  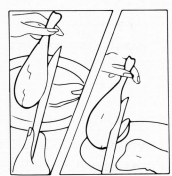

Cornbread Dressing

(photograph on page 315)

HANDS-ON **30 MINUTES**   TOTAL **1 HOUR, 15 MINUTES**   SERVES **15**

I am not a violent person, but I would fight someone who tries to tell me that "stuffing" is better than cornbread dressing. Or God forbid they follow their argument up with, "They are really just the same thing. I hardly notice any difference." Better just to bar the door.

4 cups coarsely crumbled leftover
   biscuits

4 cups coarsely crumbled cornbread

1 cup chopped celery (from 3 stalks)

½ cup chopped yellow onion
   (from 1 onion)

¾ teaspoon kosher salt

½ teaspoon black pepper

1 tablespoon chopped fresh or
   dried sage

2 cups chicken or turkey broth,
   warmed

⅓ cup (2 ⅔ ounces) salted butter,
   melted

1 cup whole milk

1   Preheat the oven to 350°F. Stir together the biscuits, cornbread, celery, onion, salt, pepper, and sage in a large bowl. Add the hot broth, and stir well. Stir in the butter and milk. Pour into a greased 13- x 9-inch baking dish.

2   Bake in the preheated oven until the top is well browned and the dressing is set, about 45 minutes.

Cranberry Salad

(photograph on page 315)

HANDS-ON **25 MINUTES**   TOTAL **8 HOURS, 25 MINUTES,**
INCLUDING CHILLING TIME   SERVES **16**

Over the years, I have realized that most people have very strong feelings about their traditional Thanksgiving dinners. This point was really driven home when I made fun of my closest friend Jincy's cranberry congealed salad. Jincy was so offended she didn't speak to me for a good week. The only reason she finally spoke to me again was because I agreed to try it. Then she made me admit, with no fingers crossed, that it was delicious. I did exactly what she asked and admitted it was delicious, but what she doesn't know is that now I serve it at my own Thanksgivings. Let's just keep that between us.

2 oranges

1 (12-ounce) package fresh cranberries

3 (3-ounce) packages orange-
   flavored gelatin

1 cup granulated sugar

3 cups boiling water

2 tablespoons fresh lemon juice
   (from 1 lemon)

⅛ teaspoon table salt

1 ½ cups finely chopped celery
   (from 4 stalks)

1 cup crushed pineapple, undrained

½ cup chopped toasted pecans
   (or more if desired)

1   Grate the zest from the oranges, and place the zest in a food processor. Add the cranberries, and pulse until finely chopped, about 20 times. Peel and section the oranges; coarsely chop the orange sections.

2   Dissolve the gelatin and sugar in 3 cups boiling water in a large bowl. Stir in the lemon juice and salt. Add the cranberry mixture, chopped oranges, celery, pineapple, and pecans. Pour into a lightly greased 12-cup Bundt pan or gelatin mold. Cover and chill until set, at least 8 hours.

Note

The salad can be made at least
2 days before serving.

Minnie's Sweet Potato Pone

HANDS-ON **25 MINUTES**   TOTAL **1 HOUR, 10 MINUTES**   SERVES **18**

Minnie helped raise my daddy, and then she helped raise my brothers and me. Minnie didn't cook a whole lot, but what she did cook was sheer perfection. The finest yeast rolls ever. Beef stew, tuna salad, and this sweet potato pone. Minnie lived to be 103 years old, and she retired at 100. She used to tell me she thought she'd lived so long because God had forgotten about her. Minnie was one of the finest women I have had the good fortune to know. It is amazing how making a special recipe can bring back a flood of joy and love. Every time I make Minnie's recipe, I can hear her talking to me, and all is right with the world.

6 cups grated sweet potatoes
   (from 2 large sweet potatoes)
1/4 cup (about 1 1/8 ounces)
   all-purpose flour
2 cups granulated sugar
1 1/3 cups whole milk

2/3 cup (5 1/3 ounces) salted
   butter, melted
2 tablespoons molasses
1/2 teaspoon ground nutmeg
1/2 teaspoon ground cinnamon
1 cup chopped pecans
6 large eggs

1 Preheat the oven to 350°F. Toss together the sweet potatoes and flour in a large bowl until the potatoes are fully coated. Add the sugar, milk, butter, molasses, nutmeg, cinnamon, pecans, and eggs, and stir to combine. Pour into a greased 13- x 9-inch baking pan.

2 Bake in the preheated oven until firm and set in the middle, about 45 minutes. Serve warm.

Simple Pecan-Green Bean Casserole

(photograph on page 320)

HANDS-ON **30 MINUTES**   TOTAL **55 MINUTES,**
INCLUDING BUTTERMILK WHITE SAUCE   SERVES **12**

This is the high-class cousin of the green bean casserole that usually starts with a can of cream of something, cans of green beans, and a can of fried onions. Sometimes it's good to hang out with the fancier cousin, and this is one of those times.

2 cups crispy fried onions
   (such as French's), crushed
1 cup panko (Japanese-style
   breadcrumbs)
1 cup chopped pecans

3 pounds fresh green beans,
   trimmed
Buttermilk White Sauce
   (recipe follows)
1 ½ cups sautéed mushrooms
   (see below)

1 Preheat the oven to 350°F. Arrange the French fried onions, panko, and chopped pecans in an even layer in a 15- x 10-inch jelly-roll pan.

2 Bake in the preheated oven for 8 to 10 minutes or until toasted, stirring after 5 minutes.

3 Cook the green beans in boiling salted water to cover 4 to 6 minutes or until crisp-tender; drain. (Do not plunge the beans into ice water.)

4 Prepare the Buttermilk White Sauce as directed. Gently toss together the warm green beans and sautéed mushrooms, and spoon onto a serving platter. Top with the Buttermilk White Sauce, and sprinkle with the toasted pecan mixture.

SAUTÉED MUSHROOMS Heat 1 tablespoon olive oil in a skillet over medium-high; add 1 pound sliced cremini mushrooms, and cook without stirring until they just start to brown, about 3 minutes. Continue to cook, stirring, 2 to 3 more minutes. **Makes about 1 ¼ cups**

Buttermilk White Sauce

Follow the directions for this sauce to the letter. If you add the milk and the buttermilk at the same time, the sauce will curdle. Once that happens, there is no bringing this baby back. The secret to this flavorful white sauce is the Ranch dressing mix. (Ok, it's true, we got snobby about canned goods in traditional green bean casseroles only to turn around and sneak in an envelope of seasoning mix in this remake.)

½ cup (4 ounces) salted butter

½ cup (about 2 ¼ ounces)
   all-purpose flour

3 cups whole milk

1 cup whole buttermilk

2 tablespoons Ranch dressing mix

½ teaspoon table salt

½ teaspoon black pepper

Melt the butter in a medium-size heavy saucepan over medium; whisk in the flour until smooth. Cook 1 minute, whisking constantly. Gradually whisk in the whole milk; cook over medium, whisking constantly, 3 to 4 minutes or until the mixture is thickened and bubbly. Remove from the heat, and whisk in the buttermilk, dressing mix, salt, and pepper. **Makes about 4 cups**

Note

The sauce can be made up to 2 days ahead. Prepare the recipe as directed; cover and chill in an airtight container. Whisk in 2 tablespoons milk, and microwave at HIGH 1 minute, stirring at 30-second intervals.

Chocolate-Bourbon Pecan Pie

HANDS-ON **15 MINUTES**   TOTAL **2 HOURS, 10 MINUTES**   SERVES **12 TO 16**

Lagniappe is a Louisiana term for a little extra surprise. This pie is all that...a bag of chocolate chips and a bottle of bourbon! For years, I ate classic pecan pie and was completely satisfied, but I had no idea what my life was missing until I tasted this recipe. I guarantee you will have a similar epiphany.

1 (14.1-ounce) package refrigerated
  piecrusts

3 cups chopped toasted pecans

2 cups semisweet chocolate chips

2 cups dark corn syrup

1 cup granulated sugar

1 cup packed light brown sugar

½ cup (4 ounces) bourbon or water

8 large eggs

½ cup (4 ounces) salted butter,
  melted

4 teaspoons plain white cornmeal

4 teaspoons vanilla extract

1 teaspoon table salt

1 Preheat the oven to 325°F. Fit 1 piecrust into each of 2 (9-inch) deep-dish pie plates according to the package directions; fold the edges under, and crimp. Sprinkle the pecans and chocolate evenly onto the bottom of the piecrusts.

2 Stir together the corn syrup, granulated sugar, brown sugar, and bourbon in a large saucepan, and bring to a boil over medium. Cook, stirring constantly, 3 minutes. Remove from the heat.

3 Whisk together the eggs, butter, cornmeal, vanilla, and salt. Gradually whisk one-fourth of the hot corn syrup mixture into the egg mixture; add to the remaining hot corn syrup mixture, whisking constantly. Pour the filling evenly into the prepared piecrusts.

4 Bake in the preheated oven for 55 minutes or until set; cool the pies completely on a wire rack, about 1 hour.

'Twas the
Night Before...
FONDUE PARTY

Beef Fondue | Warm Mustard Sauce
Herbed Green Sauce | Cheese Fondue
Double Chocolate Fondue
Buttermilk Pound Cake

'TWAS THE NIGHT BEFORE...FONDUE PARTY

MENU FOR 20

My sister-in-law Elizabeth met a boy at a barbecue festival in Memphis, Tennessee. He was from Texas, and the next thing we knew she moved there and up and married him. I wasn't a fan. Not of the boy, my new brother-in-law, but of Texas. Maybe it's that people from Texas seemed a little too uppity for my taste. Whenever someone said, "Everything's bigger in Texas," I would whisper under my breath, "Well maybe but everything is better in Mississippi."

I didn't want to like her new Texas family. I was pretty insistent on that notion until the year she stayed in Texas for Christmas. I couldn't imagine anything worse, but she was pleased as punch not to be coming home. They had won her over with Christmas Eve fondue. My harsh feelings toward her new state started to fade after hearing about all that fondue. It was a brilliant idea.

No one has a minute to spare during the holidays. Finding time to prepare an elaborate meal for both Christmas Eve and Christmas Day is stressful. Enter fondue. It's simple as hell, and you don't really even have to cook it. Your family does the work. Just prepare a few sauces, cut up some meat and vegetables, and you're done. It's also a nice way for family to connect. Everyone has to sit close. I cannot imagine a more perfect excuse to blow the dust off that 1970s fondue pot relegated to the garage. Guests of all ages can participate and join in on the the cooking and eating.

It's true, fondue softened my heart toward Texas. After several trips to Houston, its fancy restaurants, and Neiman Marcus, followed by weeks of fishing in Rockport, my stone-cold heart had turned to mush for the Lone Star State. I get it now. Texans aren't egomaniacs. Everything is bigger in Texas. It's a place of big hearts, big gatherings, and big personalities, and now my sister-in-law has a really big fondue pot for when the Heiskells come to visit.

Beef Fondue

HANDS-ON **35 MINUTES**   TOTAL **40 MINUTES**   SERVES **20**

Fondue is a great icebreaker. It's the original communal dining. Make sure you make the sauces and the oil before your guests arrive so you can join in on the fun too.

3 pounds beef tenderloin or boneless
   sirloin steak, trimmed
Clarified Butter (recipe follows)

³/₄ cup good-quality olive oil
Warm Mustard Sauce (page 330)
Herbed Green Sauce (page 330)

1 Cut the trimmed beef tenderloin into ¾-inch cubes. Cover and chill the meat until ready to use.

2 About 20 minutes before serving, heat the Clarified Butter and oil together in a medium saucepan over medium until the mixture begins to bubble. Transfer to a 2-quart fondue pot or saucepan. (The mixture should not be more than about 2 inches deep.)

3 Heat the butter mixture on a fondue stand until it begins to bubble. Use fondue forks to cook the beef 2 to 3 minutes, or to desired doneness. Serve with the Warm Mustard Sauce and Herbed Green Sauce.

Note

Guests may be provided with individual dishes of
several kinds of dipping sauces, or a communal pot
where all may dip into it. The butter-oil mixture
may be reused; keep refrigerated.

CLARIFIED BUTTER Melt 2 cups (1 pound) salted butter in a small saucepan over low without stirring. Remove from the heat, and let stand 10 minutes. (The butter will separate and the milk solids will settle to the bottom of the saucepan.) Skim the butter fat from the top; discard the milk solids. Place several layers of cheesecloth in a strainer; strain the butter fat through the cheesecloth into a small bowl. **Makes 1 cup**

Warm Mustard Sauce

HANDS-ON **5 MINUTES**   TOTAL **5 MINUTES**   SERVES **16**

Three ingredients and a whisk—you won't hear me complaining about this. It does need to be made the night before serving but—back to the three ingredients and a whisk—no complaints here.

3 tablespoons Dijon mustard

3 tablespoons Worcestershire sauce

10 tablespoons (5 ounces) unsalted butter

Whisk together the mustard, Worcestershire sauce, and butter in a small saucepan. Cook over low, stirring constantly, until the butter is melted and the sauce is hot. (Do not boil.) Serve hot. Keep the sauce warm in a double boiler.

Herbed Green Sauce

HANDS-ON **10 MINUTES**   TOTAL **10 MINUTES, PLUS OVERNIGHT CHILLING**   SERVES **18**

This sauce goes well with beef fondue and more. It is lovely mixed with cold poached chicken for yet another chicken salad variation. What are we up to now…1,004 recipes? It is lovely served with cold shrimp or as a dip for crudité too.

1 teaspoon dried basil

1 teaspoon dried tarragon

1 small garlic clove, crushed

1 teaspoon dried chervil (optional)

½ cup finely chopped fresh flat-leaf parsley

½ cup mayonnaise

½ cup sour cream

1 tablespoon fresh lemon juice (from 1 lemon)

½ teaspoon kosher salt

Dash of ground nutmeg

Crush the basil, tarragon, garlic, and, if desired, chervil in a small bowl, using a wooden spoon, to make a paste. Stir in the parsley, mayonnaise, sour cream, lemon juice, salt, and nutmeg. Chill overnight before serving to allow the flavors to blend.

Fondue Parties

Fondue parties have become a popular type of entertainment, especially among the young marrieds. They're great ice breakers and suit spontaneous entertaining and casual settings where space and equipment are at a premium.

A simple, practically pre-prepared menu leaves the hostess free to mingle with the convivial gathering. Then when the time is come, guests gather around the pots (do borrow enough extras from friends), grab a fork, and the dipping begins: beef sizzled in hot oil, bread cubes swished in bubbly cheese, or fruit tidbits swirled in creamy chocolate.

The gaiety of the party is assured before the hostess buys her first pound of cheese or beef — for how can you avoid being friendly with others whose fondue forks are being stirred in unison with your own?

Cheese Fondue

HANDS-ON **20 MINUTES**   TOTAL **20 MINUTES**   SERVES **20**

French bread is the go-to cheese fondue dipper, but fresh vegetables are a fun addition. Sliced peppers, blanched broccoli and asparagus, quartered mushrooms ... the list goes on and on, so be sure to invite plenty of hungry friends. Always use high-quality Swiss cheese for the best results.

1 ½ pounds Swiss cheese, shredded
(about 6 cups)

2 tablespoons cornstarch

2 cups dry white wine

⅛ teaspoon ground white pepper

⅛ teaspoon ground nutmeg

2 tablespoons (1 ounce) kirsch
(cherry brandy), brandy, or cognac

Bite-size pieces of French bread,
toasted

1 Toss together the cheese and cornstarch in a large bowl. Pour the wine into a medium saucepan, and place over low; cook until air bubbles rise to the surface, about 8 minutes. (Do not boil.) Gradually add the cheese, stirring constantly until each addition is melted before adding more. Continue stirring until the mixture is bubbling lightly. Add the pepper, nutmeg, and kirsch; stir to combine.

2 Pour into a warmed fondue pot. Keep the heat under the pot very low. (Do not let the fondue boil.) Use fondue forks to dip the bread into the melted cheese mixture.

Double Chocolate Fondue

HANDS-ON **35 MINUTES**   TOTAL **35 MINUTES**   SERVES **37**

When serving chocolate fondue, make sure you are with your most nonjudgmental friends. You know, the type of friends who won't count how many marshmallows, pretzel rods, or pound cake chunks you dipped and devoured. Don't skim on the dippers; this is chocolate fondue. The more the merrier.

FONDUE

8 ounces semisweet chocolate,
   chopped

4 ounces German's sweet chocolate
   baking bar, chopped

3/4 cup whole milk

Dash of ground cinnamon (optional)

DIPPERS

Buttermilk Pound Cake cubes
   (page 337)

Fresh pineapple chunks

Canned mandarin orange sections

Banana chunks

Other fresh fruit

Marshmallows

Maraschino cherries with stems

Ladyfinger biscotti

1 Combine the semisweet chocolate, German's chocolate, milk, and cinnamon, if desired, in the top of a double boiler. Place over gently simmering water, and stir until the sauce is completely smooth.

2 Pour into a fondue pot, small slow cooker, or chafing dish. Keep warm while serving. (If heated longer than 30 minutes, add additional milk for a proper consistency.) Serve with the assorted dippers.

Buttermilk Pound Cake

HANDS-ON **20 MINUTES**   TOTAL **3 HOURS, 10 MINUTES**   SERVES **32**

The first step is the most crucial part of this recipe. You must make sure the butter, shortening, and sugar are well creamed and as fluffy as a cloud. Start the mixture in a stand mixer, and then eat a bowl of cereal, fold a load of laundry, or feed the dog. You have plenty of time. Then, and only then, move on to the next step. Your pound cake's life depends on it.

½ cup (4 ounces) unsalted butter, softened, plus more for pans

½ cup shortening

3 cups granulated sugar

5 large eggs

2 teaspoons vanilla extract

3 cups (about 12 ¾ ounces) all-purpose flour, plus more for the pans

½ teaspoon baking soda

½ teaspoon table salt

1 cup whole buttermilk

1 Preheat the oven to 325°F. Beat the butter, shortening, and sugar with a stand mixer at medium speed until light and fluffy, about 5 minutes, stopping to scrape down the sides as needed. Add the eggs, 1 at a time, beating well after each addition. Beat in the vanilla. Combine the flour, baking soda, and salt in a medium bowl; add the flour mixture to the butter mixture alternately with the buttermilk, beginning and ending with the flour mixture. Beat at low speed just until blended after each addition. Pour into 2 greased and floured 8-inch square pans.

2 Bake in the preheated oven until a wooden pick inserted in the center comes out clean, about 40 minutes, testing for doneness after 35 minutes. Cool in the pans 10 minutes. Run a knife around the edges of the pans; remove the cake from the pans, and cool completely on a wire rack, about 2 hours. Cut into 1-inch cubes.

Note

For a traditional pound cake, bake in a 10-inch tube pan. Bake at 300°F for 1 ½ hours, testing for doneness after 1 hour and 20 minutes.

CHRISTMAS
NIGHT FEAST

Shrimp Creole · Lemon Rice
Chocolate Bread Pudding with Whiskey Sauce
Hot Boozy Coffee

CHRISTMAS NIGHT FEAST

Just like everyone else on the planet, the holidays tucker me out! I always wait until the very last minute to shop. I wrap presents on Christmas Eve. I cook for days on end. I attend and host numerous holiday parties, not to mention that my catering company is in full swing. While I do love every minute of the frantic pace, I'll be honest. . .no one is happier on Christmas afternoon than I am. It's my time to have fun.

After all the dishes and food from lunch have been put up, all the presents opened and wrapping paper, ribbon, and tissue paper burned to ash in the fireplace, my work is done. It's my time to finally relax. So, of course, that's when I invite my best friends and their children over for a party.

It's a BYOB, serve-yourself-from-the-stove sort of affair. The kids get to show off their favorite new gifts and we get to wear the new, stylish clothes that Santa brought. Sitting by the fire, sipping wine with my friends, and reveling in the fact that we survived Christmas once again is like a healing balm. (We also never fail to declare how next year we will be more organized so things won't be so hectic.)

This is when you pull out one of those favorite make-ahead dishes you froze weeks ago. Just pull it out the day before and thaw it in the fridge. It's also the perfect time to artfully arrange on a tray all of those goodies from the half-eaten boxes, bags, and tins people delivered to your door over the holidays. If necessary, add a can of nuts to the snack mix your neighbor brought to bulk it up. Cube that leftover pound cake and serve it with wooden picks and a big bowl of whipped cream. Add those last four bourbon balls that have been taunting you to the mix too; it's time for them to go. Just put it all out, and let everyone help themselves. Tonight is about relaxing with friends. (And letting them inhale the remnants of the holidays so you have less to wrap up, toss, or devour tomorrow simply because it's still there. Yes, your waistline thanks me.)

Shrimp Creole

HANDS-ON **30 MINUTES**   TOTAL **1 HOUR,**
INCLUDING LEMON RICE   SERVES **8**

Many traditional Louisiana cookbooks call this Creole "sauce piquant." It is an easy one-pot dish, but it's sophisticated enough to serve at even the most special occasions. The Creole sauce can be frozen for months. Before serving, thaw the sauce, bring it to a boil, add the shrimp, and cook until the shrimp are just done. Be very careful not to overcook the shrimp. There is nothing more disappointing than a beautiful Creole with rubbery shrimp.

2 medium onions, chopped

1 cup chopped green bell pepper
   (from 1 bell pepper)

1 cup chopped celery (from 3 stalks)

2 teaspoons minced garlic

6 tablespoons olive oil

6 tablespoons (about 1 ³/₄ ounces)
   all-purpose flour

2 (28-ounce) cans crushed tomatoes

1 cup chicken broth

2 teaspoons Cajun seasoning

1 teaspoon table salt

¹/₂ teaspoon cayenne pepper

4 bay leaves

2 pounds raw medium shrimp, peeled

Lemon Rice (page 342)

Chopped fresh parsley (optional)

1 Sauté the onions, bell pepper, celery, and garlic in hot olive oil in a large skillet over medium 5 minutes or until the onion is tender; gradually stir in the flour until smooth. Stir in the tomatoes, broth, Cajun seasoning, salt, cayenne pepper, and bay leaves.

2 Cover, reduce the heat to low, and cook, stirring occasionally, 20 minutes. Stir in the shrimp, and cook 5 more minutes or until the shrimp turn pink. Remove and discard the bay leaves. Serve over the Lemon Rice. Garnish with chopped parsley, if desired.

Lemon Rice

(photograph on page 341)

HANDS-ON **15 MINUTES**   TOTAL **40 MINUTES**   SERVES **8**

Lemon Rice pairs beautifully with any seafood dish, but is also a lovely partner for roasted chicken or pork tenderloin. This versatile, understated rice dish is sure to become one of your recipe staples.

1 cup uncooked jasmine rice

1 tablespoon extra-virgin olive oil

½ cup finely chopped yellow onion
   (from 1 medium onion)

½ cup coarsely chopped fresh mint

1 tablespoon lemon zest, plus 4 teaspoons
   fresh juice (from 1 lemon)

¼ cup chopped fresh flat-leaf parsley

1 teaspoon kosher salt

½ cup pine nuts, toasted (optional)

1 Bring a medium saucepan of water to a boil over medium-high. Stir in the rice; cover and reduce the heat to medium-low, and simmer until the rice is tender, about 20 minutes. Pour the rice into a fine mesh strainer, and drain. Rinse with cold water until cool.

2 Heat 1 teaspoon of the oil in a small saucepan over medium. Add the onion, and cook, stirring occasionally, until translucent, 2 to 3 minutes. Place the rice and onion in a large bowl; add the mint, lemon zest, lemon juice, parsley, salt, remaining 2 teaspoons oil, and, if desired, the pine nuts, and toss. Serve warm or at room temperature.

Leftovers

After the hustle and bustle of the holidays, everyone is ready for a night off. Yet for some reason, leftovers always seem to get a bad rap. Take a cue from swanky restaurants by elevating your homecooked overflow with a dose of panache. Pretty packaging—a simple craft box, an herb sprig, and a tag with reheating instructions—tied up with a bow makes any offering feel extra special. Just like that, leftovers become "luxeovers" that departing guests will truly appreciate.

Chocolate Bread Pudding with Whiskey Sauce

HANDS-ON **30 MINUTES**   TOTAL **3 HOURS, 15 MINUTES,**
INCLUDING WHISKEY SAUCE   SERVES **8 TO 10**

Just because this recipe calls for French bread cubes doesn't mean you have to use French bread cubes. You are the boss of this recipe, and no one can stop you from using donuts or croissants instead. I dare you!

¼ cup (2 ounces) unsalted butter

7 cups French bread cubes

2 cups whipping cream

1 cup whole milk

8 (1-ounce) bittersweet chocolate
   squares, chopped

5 egg yolks, lightly beaten

⅔ cup packed light brown sugar

1 teaspoon vanilla extract

Whiskey Sauce (recipe follows)

Chocolate shavings

1 Melt the butter in a large skillet over medium. Add the bread; cook, stirring constantly, 3 minutes or until golden. Transfer to a greased 13- x 9-inch baking dish.

2 Bring the cream and milk to a boil over medium in the skillet. Remove from the heat; whisk in the chocolate, egg yolks, brown sugar, and vanilla. Pour over the bread cubes; let stand 30 minutes.

3 Preheat the oven to 325°F. Cover the baking dish with aluminum foil; cut 6 small holes in the foil to allow steam to escape. Place the baking dish in a roasting pan. Add hot water to the pan to a depth of 1 ½ inches. Bake 1 hour and 45 minutes or until set. Remove from the water bath. Cool 30 minutes on a wire rack. Serve warm with the Whiskey Sauce and chocolate shavings, if desired.

Whiskey Sauce

1 ½ cups whole milk

½ cup (4 ounces) salted butter

1 cup granulated sugar

3 tablespoons cornstarch

¼ cup water

½ cup (4 ounces) bourbon

1 Cook the milk, butter, and sugar in a heavy saucepan over low, stirring often, until the butter melts and the sugar dissolves.

2 Combine the cornstarch and ¼ cup water, stirring until smooth. Add to the butter mixture; stir in the bourbon. Bring to a boil over medium, stirring constantly; boil, stirring constantly, 1 minute. **Makes about 3 ¼ cups**

Hot Boozy Coffee

HANDS-ON **10 MINUTES**   TOTAL **10 MINUTES**   SERVES **8**

I have always preferred to drink my dessert. This dessert coffee has a serious kick. Feel free to play around with liqueurs you love. It's also very fun to fill a bowl with airplane-size bottles of liquor so your guests can choose for themselves.

To set up a really, truly fun boozy coffee bar, you really need only a few things. Your guests can mix and match as they please, and all you have to do is set everything up to make it look delicious and inviting. Arrange all the ingredients on a coffee bar table or cart. If you want, you can place the recipe guidelines on note cards just to give your guests an idea about where to start.

8 cups hot brewed coffee

1 ½ cups (12 ounces) Irish whiskey

2 cups (16 ounces) coffee liqueur (such as Kahlúa)

2 cups (16 ounces) amaretto (almond liqueur)

1 ½ cups simple syrup

2 cups whipped cream

1 cup whipping cream or half-and-half

Ground cinnamon

Whole nutmeg, for grating

Cinnamon sticks

Unsweetened cocoa

Lemon peel twists

Orange peel twists

Chocolate curls

IRISH COFFEE Combine ½ cup coffee, 3 tablespoons Irish whiskey, and 2 tablespoons simple syrup in a mug. Top with a spoonful of whipped cream, a sprinkle of cinnamon, and garnish with a cinnamon stick.

KAHLÚA COFFEE Combine ½ cup coffee and ¼ cup coffee liqueur in a mug. Top with whipped cream and a sprinkle of cocoa. Garnish with the chocolate curls and an orange twist.

AMARETTO COFFEE Combine ½ cup coffee, ¼ cup amaretto, and 2 tablespoons cream or half-and-half in a mug. Top with a sprinkle of nutmeg, and garnish with a lemon twist.

New Year's Eve

She-Crab Soup

The Plantation Club Salad with
Lemon-Mustard Dressing

Standing Rib Roast

Alabama Spoonbread

Creamed Spinach with Crunchy Topping

Bananas Foster

NEW YEAR'S EVE

New Year's Eve is amateur night if you ask me. Those barricaded street parties and ball-dropping mobfests appeal to people who rarely go out the rest of the year. With so much hype, recluses feel compelled to crawl out from under their rocks, put on makeup and sequins, and paint the town. Don't get me wrong, I'm truly excited for them. I hope they realize how much fun going out can be and will continue right on whooping it up for the rest of the year. I can tell you one thing though: You will not find me among them. For me, this night is reserved for my very closest friends and the finest, most decadent food I can muster up.

It's the very first party of the year so of course I pull out all the stops. I put into service my best china and crystal, pretty place mats that sparkle in the glow of candlelight, and crisply starched linen napkins in handsome napkin rings. No party setup is complete without a few simple flower arrangements. Make sure the centerpieces are low enough so that your guests can talk over them. I like to use snowy white roses as an elegant backdrop to all the shimmer and shine.

A standing rib roast is beyond luxurious; it makes an impression. The first time I attempted to make it I was terrified. It wasn't until my mother-in-law, Babo, cooked one to serve as a simple family dinner that I realized it was nothing more than a big ol' bone-in steak. I also realized that "trussing" was as easy as sewing on a button!

With my mind at ease, I decided to make New Year's Eve my first attempt at the roast. My confidence grew as I cooked, remembering Babo's ease with the monster roast. No one was more surprised than I was when it turned out perfectly. Lord, I was puffed up and proud. It made my year. I always end this dinner party by thanking my friends for all they do for us and send each one home with my hair-of-the-dog care package. It includes my Bloody Mary mix, vodka, and all the fixings to ease any hangover that the first morning of the New Year might bring.

She-Crab Soup

HANDS-ON **10 MINUTES**   TOTAL **45 MINUTES**   SERVES **7**

I have had just a few dining experiences I can look back on and honestly say that I remember every single aspect of the meal. One in particular was when Luke and I were newlyweds and visiting Charleston. Luke's mother's best friend, Bessie, invited us to her home on The Battery. I can still recall every detail of that experience, from the intricate pattern of the antique rug to how cold, crisp, and delicious the wine was. Bessie started the meal with she-crab soup and it made an incredible impression on me. Most days I cannot remember my children's names, but I will never forget that soup.

½ cup (4 ounces) salted butter

¼ cup finely chopped yellow
  onion (from 1 onion)

⅓ cup (about 1½ ounces)
  all-purpose flour

6 cups whole milk

2 tablespoons sherry

1 teaspoon table salt

1 teaspoon paprika

¼ teaspoon ground white pepper

8 ounces fresh crabmeat,
  picked over

3 ounces crab roe or yolks of
  3 hard-cooked eggs, grated

Paprika, chopped chives (optional)

1 Melt the butter in a large Dutch oven over medium-low. Add the onion, and cook, stirring occasionally, 3 minutes. Add the flour, and cook, stirring occasionally, 1 minute.

2 Stir in the milk, sherry, salt, paprika, and white pepper. Simmer over low 25 to 30 minutes. Just before serving, stir in the crabmeat and crab roe. Garnish with paprika and chopped chives, if desired.

Note

Authentic she-crab soup is made from what is considered to be the sweeter meat of female crabs heavy with roe on their shell exteriors. The coral-colored roe gives the soup its distinctive flavor and a blushing hue. Today, law demands that crabs harvested with roe on the outside be returned to the water. If you are lucky enough to open the shell of a crab with the roe inside, you're in luck! Stir in that delicacy to experience this iconic Charleston soup.

The Plantation Club Salad with Lemon-Mustard Dressing

HANDS-ON **25 MINUTES**   TOTAL **25 MINUTES**   SERVES **6**

The addition of the mustard to this vinaigrette acts as the marriage counselor between two things that don't want to go together: oil and vinegar. The mustard is an emulsifier, or tie that binds, which ensures that the vinaigrette is velvety-smooth instead of beady and broken.

½ cup fresh lemon juice (from
    4 lemons)
2 teaspoons spicy brown mustard
1 teaspoon dry English mustard
    (such as Colman's)
1 ½ teaspoons kosher salt
¼ teaspoon ground white pepper
1 teaspoon Worcestershire sauce
2 teaspoons finely chopped
    fresh chives

1 teaspoon finely chopped fresh
    tarragon
1 teaspoon finely chopped fresh basil
1 cup extra-virgin olive oil
8 cups mixed salad greens (from
    1 [5-ounce] container)
2 (14-ounce) cans quartered artichoke
    hearts, drained
1 (14-ounce) can hearts of palm, drained
    and cut into 1-inch-thick slices
Black pepper

1 Whisk together the lemon juice, spicy brown mustard, English mustard, salt, white pepper, Worcestershire sauce, chives, tarragon, and basil in a large bowl. Gradually whisk in the olive oil until well blended. Transfer the dressing to a container with a lid. Cover and chill until ready to serve.

2 Drizzle ⅓ cup of the dressing on the salad greens in a large bowl; toss well. (Refrigerate the remaining dressing for up to 2 weeks.) Divide the salad among serving plates; top evenly with the artichoke hearts and the hearts of palm. Sprinkle with the black pepper.

1972 SOUTHERN LIVING PARTY COOKBOOK ORIGINAL

Wine Selection Guide

TYPE OF WINE	SPECIFIC WINE	SERVE WITH	TEMPERATURE	WHEN TO SERVE
Appetizer	Sherry, dry Vermouth, dry Port	Appetizers, nuts, cheese	Chilled, room temperature over time	Before dinner
Table Wines (white)	Rhine, Chablis, Sauterne, Light Muscat, Sauterne, Riesling, White Chianti	Fish, seafood, poultry, cheese, lamb, veal, eggs, lighter foods, pork (except ham)	Chilled	With dinner
Table Wines (red)	Rosé	Curry patio parties, Chinese food, any food	Slightly chilled	With dinner, any time, with or without food
	Claret	Game, Italian food, beef, Hawaiian food	Slightly chilled	With dinner
	Chianti, Vino Rosso	Red meat, cheese, roasts, game, Italian food	Slightly chilled	With dinner
	Burgundy	Cheese, Italian food, game, ham, heartier foods, roasts, steaks	Slightly chilled	With dinner, any time, with or without food
Sparkling Wines	Champagne, dry	Appetizers, fish, seafood, poultry, main courses, desserts, cheese, any festive meal	Chilled	Any time with or without food
	Sparkling Burgundy	Appetizers, main courses, roasts, game, desserts	Chilled	Any time
Dessert Wines	Port; Muscatel, Tokay; Champagne (sweet); Sherry (cream); Madeira, sweet; Sauterne; Marsala; Malaga	Desserts, fruit, nuts, cheeses, cakes, pastries	Cool room temperature	After dinner, with dessert

Standing Rib Roast

HANDS-ON **15 MINUTES**   TOTAL **1 HOUR, 40 MINUTES**   SERVES **6**

A standing rib roast is the hallmark of a special occasion. It is a very expensive cut of meat so overcooking it would be a disgrace. Please purchase a meat thermometer; it will be your best friend during this cooking process. See detailed carving instructions on page 316.

1 (3-rib) standing rib roast
(about 8 ½ pounds)

2 ½ teaspoons kosher salt
1 teaspoon black pepper

1 Preheat the oven to 450°F. Season the roast with the salt and pepper. Place the roast, fat side up, on a rack in a large roasting pan. Insert a meat thermometer so the bulb reaches the center of the thickest part, but does not rest in the fat or on the bone.

2 Bake, uncovered, in the preheated oven 20 minutes. Reduce the temperature to 350°F, and bake until the thermometer registers 125°F, about 1 hour and 5 minutes. Wrap the roast in foil. Let rest until the temperature rises to 130°F to 135°F, about 8 minutes, before serving.

Tip

Have the butcher remove the chine bone from the roast to make carving easier. This roasting time applies to 3-rib roasts. Rolled beef rib roasts require about the same cooking time. For longer cut rib roasts, the cooking time should be reduced to about 5 minutes per pound.

Alabama Spoonbread

(photograph on page 355)

HANDS-ON **20 MINUTES**   TOTAL **50 MINUTES**   SERVES **8**

If you ask me, this is the Southern equivalent of Yorkshire pudding. It's a side dish that pairs exceptionally well with beef, but also with seafood or pork.

1 cup (about 5 ¾ ounces) finely ground plain yellow cornmeal

1 ¾ cups boiling water

1 tablespoon salted butter, plus more for serving

1 ½ teaspoons kosher salt

4 large eggs, separated

½ cup whole milk

½ cup (about 2 ⅛ ounces) all-purpose flour

1 tablespoon granulated sugar

2 teaspoons baking powder

1 Preheat the oven to 400°F. Sprinkle the cornmeal over the boiling water in a large bowl. Add the butter and salt; stir until the mixture is thick. Cool about 5 minutes. Add the egg yolks and milk; whisk until blended. Combine the flour, sugar, and baking powder in separate bowl; add to the batter, mixing well.

2 Beat the egg whites in a separate medium bowl with an electric mixer at high speed until stiff (but not dry) peaks form; gently fold into the batter. Pour into a greased 12- x 8-inch (2-quart) baking or soufflé dish.

3 Bake in the preheated oven until a knife inserted in the center comes out clean, 30 to 35 minutes. Serve immediately with plenty of butter.

PARTY RULE NO. 12

Safety rules

Everyone loves a great time, but when it is obvious a partygoer has overindulged, you have a measure of responsibility to keep them from driving. Take their keys, put them in a cab, or let them sleep it off in the guest room, but never let an inebriated guest get behind the wheel of a car and jeopardize their safety and the safety of others.

Creamed Spinach with Crunchy Topping

(photograph on page 355)

HANDS-ON **15 MINUTES** TOTAL **45 MINUTES** SERVES **9**

You are more than welcome to make your own breadcrumb topping for this delightful side. I freeze stale bread just for this occasion. When I need breadcrumbs, I pull the bread out of the freezer, place it in a food processor with a little melted butter and fresh herbs, give it a quick pulse, and voilà: herbed breadcrumbs.

3 (10-ounce) packages frozen leaf
  spinach, thawed
1 (8-ounce) package cream cheese,
  softened
½ cup whipping cream
6 tablespoons (3 ounces) unsalted
  butter, melted

½ teaspoon table salt
½ teaspoon black pepper
⅛ teaspoon ground nutmeg
1 tablespoon lemon zest (from 1 lemon)
1 cup croutons, coarsely crushed

1 Drain the spinach well, pressing between paper towels to remove excess moisture. Place in a bowl; stir in the cream cheese, whipping cream, and 3 tablespoons of the butter. Stir in the salt, pepper, nutmeg, and lemon zest. Spoon into a buttered 8-inch square baking dish. Cover and refrigerate until ready to bake. (This may be prepared in the morning of the day it is served.)

2 Preheat the oven to 350°F. Sprinkle the crushed croutons over the top and drizzle with the remaining 3 tablespoons butter. Bake, uncovered, in the preheated oven until bubbly, about 25 minutes.

Bananas Foster

HANDS-ON **15 MINUTES**   TOTAL **15 MINUTES**   SERVES **6**

This dessert got its start at the famed Brennan's Restaurant in New Orleans in the 1950s. Dole started shipping bananas into the New Orleans port, and chef Paul Blangé was challenged to create a dish to celebrate this new business. They named this flamed dessert after the then-New Orleans Crime Commissioner chairman Richard Foster, and the rest is culinary history.

6 medium bananas

1 ½ tablespoons fresh lemon juice
(from 1 lemon)

6 tablespoons (3 ounces) salted butter

¾ cup packed light brown sugar

6 tablespoons granulated sugar

6 tablespoons (3 ounces) rum

3 tablespoons (1 ½ ounces) banana
liqueur

3 tablespoons (1 ½ ounces) brandy

¾ teaspoon ground cinnamon

Vanilla ice cream

1 Peel and slice each banana diagonally into 6 pieces. Toss with the lemon juice. Melt the butter in a large skillet over medium-low. Add the brown and granulated sugars; cook, stirring constantly, until the mixture bubbles, about 6 minutes. Add the bananas; cook until slightly softened, about 1 minute. Remove from the heat.

2 Add the rum, banana liqueur, brandy, and cinnamon. Carefully ignite with a long match or lighter; let the flames die down. Return the pan to medium-high; cook, stirring occasionally, until the sauce is smooth, 1 to 2 minutes. Divide the banana mixture among 6 shallow serving bowls; top with vanilla ice cream.

Metric Equivalents

COOKING/OVEN TEMPERATURES

	Fahrenheit	Celsius	Gas Mark
Freeze Water	32° F	0° C	
Room Temp.	68° F	20° C	
Boil Water	212° F	100° C	
Bake	325° F	160° C	3
	350° F	180° C	4
	375° F	190° C	5
	400° F	200° C	6
	425° F	220° C	7
	450° F	230° C	8
Broil			Grill

LIQUID INGREDIENTS BY VOLUME

$\frac{1}{4}$ tsp					=	1 ml	
$\frac{1}{2}$ tsp					=	2 ml	
1 tsp					=	5 ml	
3 tsp	=	1 Tbsp	=	$\frac{1}{2}$ fl oz	=	15 ml	
2 Tbsp	=	$\frac{1}{8}$ cup	=	1 fl oz	=	30 ml	
4 Tbsp	=	$\frac{1}{4}$ cup	=	2 fl oz	=	60 ml	
5 $\frac{1}{3}$ Tbsp	=	$\frac{1}{3}$ cup	=	3 fl oz	=	80 ml	
8 Tbsp	=	$\frac{1}{2}$ cup	=	4 fl oz	=	120 ml	
10 $\frac{2}{3}$ Tbsp	=	$\frac{2}{3}$ cup	=	5 fl oz	=	160 ml	
12 Tbsp	=	$\frac{3}{4}$ cup	=	6 fl oz	=	180 ml	
16 Tbsp	=	1 cup	=	8 fl oz	=	240 ml	
1 pt	=	2 cups	=	16 fl oz	=	480 ml	
1 qt	=	4 cups	=	32 fl oz	=	960 ml	
				33 fl oz	=	1000 ml	= 1 l

DRY INGREDIENTS BY WEIGHT

(To convert ounces to grams, multiply the number of ounces by 30.)

1 oz	=	$\frac{1}{16}$ lb	=	30 g
4 oz	=	$\frac{1}{4}$ lb	=	120 g
8 oz	=	$\frac{1}{2}$ lb	=	240 g
12 oz	=	$\frac{3}{4}$ lb	=	360 g
16 oz	=	1 lb	=	480 g

LENGTH

(To convert inches to centimeters, multiply inches by 2.5.)

1 in				=	2.5 cm		
12 in	=	1 ft		=	30 cm		
36 in	=	3 ft	=	1 yd	=	90 cm	
40 in				=	100 cm	=	1m

EQUIVALENTS FOR DIFFERENT TYPES OF INGREDIENTS

Standard Cup	Fine Powder (ex. flour)	Grain (ex. rice)	Granular (ex. sugar)	Liquid Solids (ex. butter)	Liquid (ex. milk)
1	140 g	150 g	190 g	200 g	240 ml
$\frac{3}{4}$	105 g	113 g	143 g	150 g	180 ml
$\frac{2}{3}$	93 g	100 g	125 g	133 g	160 ml
$\frac{1}{2}$	70 g	75 g	95 g	100 g	120 ml
$\frac{1}{3}$	47 g	50 g	63 g	67 g	80 ml
$\frac{1}{4}$	35 g	38 g	48 g	50 g	60 ml
$\frac{1}{8}$	18 g	19 g	24 g	25 g	30 ml

Party Index

361

General Index

363

364

365

367

Acknowledgments

*For Sarah Virden, your grace, love, and kind spirit have made
all the difference. There is no one I would rather party with.*

I am so deeply grateful for Luke, Stott, Mary Paxton, and Lucia. Without you, none of this would be possible.

To Daddy, I am blessed beyond belief that you are mine. I couldn't ask for more in a father or friend.

To Mama, thank you for always teaching me to see the beauty that God has surrounded us with. Your creativity somehow spilled over into me and I am grateful.

To Grandmother, thank you for always setting the entertaining bar high. Lord have mercy, you are a hard act to follow.

To William, thank you for being my brother. I am in constant awe of your kind spirit.

To Parker, thank you for your constant dedication to the company and to me. I don't deserve it, but I will never take it for granted.

To Amanda, thank you for going along with all my crazy ideas and making them even better. Belly dancers, funeral sprays, and all. You are an amazing party partner, and I am grateful.

To Babo, thank you for being a mother-in-law who loves a pretty party as much as I do.

To Machelle, thank you for being my friend and making our Halloween party an epic occasion. It is just my favorite day of the year. Your excitement and passion for all things ghostly and ghoulish is contagious.

To Sid Evans, who would have thought a visit to the farm would lead to this? I am so grateful for you.

To Katherine Cobbs, thank you for giving me this most amazing opportunity. I am so grateful you are my editor but more grateful that you are my friend.

To Kara, thank you for always getting the party started with the most genius invitations and ideas. You are stupid cool, and I love you dearly.

To David, Katie, Ashley, and the Oxford Floral Staff, thank you for putting up with me, inspiring me, and loving me. I honestly don't know what in the world I would do without you all; your support has made all the difference.

To Greg, Eric, and the Garden District friends, 22 years of flowers and friendship from my mud-filled wedding to now and all the years in between—I am deeply grateful for you all.

To Kourtney and Danielle, you two are the best in the business. I would be lost and in a lot of trouble without your patience, love, and support and the all-important Google Doc. Thank you for not only selling the book but for selling the best in me.

To Anya, thank you for your genius ways. You are beyond talented, and this book is better because of you.

To Marsha and Ellen, I wouldn't be who I am without our monthly visit. Thank you for all the love.

To Debbie, you have forever changed my life and my children's lives. Thank you for all the love and support you have shown me over the years. I pray one day I can repay you.

To Ann Marie, Kenneth, and the Details family, no party would be complete without you. Thank you for the years of support and vision.

To all the clients of Elizabeth Heiskell Catering, thank you for trusting your most special party memories to us.

To all the staff members that have worked tirelessly for the company, I never took one moment of your efforts for granted. As my friend says, "the people make the party" and y'all damn sure do!